WORKING ARTIST | STARVING ARTIST

ARTIST | ARTIST

The New Business of Show Business

Tyler Griffin

STARVING ARTIST
COMPANY

Published by Starving Artist Company, Ltd. Liability Co.

First paperback edition published 2016.

ISBN-10:0-692-63783-4
ISBN-13:978-0-692-63783-8

Cover and Logo Designed by RhoDesign

This book is dedicated to all my fellow artists and performers. Your dedication to the arts is both courageous and inspiring. I hope this book helps to make your journey a little easier.

Working Artist, Starving Artist

The New Business of Show Business

Contents

INTRODUCTION

"Show business is a money-making joke. And I like telling jokes."

– Dolly Parton

This is not your typical "How to" guide to making a living in show business. This is a guide on how to live your fullest life while simultaneously pursuing your passions. If you are looking for a book to tell you "how to make it big in 3 easy steps" or how to become famous overnight, you're looking in the wrong place. You'll quickly learn through these pages that fame is just a by-product of success and that success is something defined by you.

This book is more than that. This book is a guide to help you define your own success, no matter what level of the entertainment business you are on. You'll learn from this book that everything you considered "concrete" is subjective and that you are the one that gets to make the rules. You'll learn that you are the one in control of your situation and that you can guide your future in show business in any direction you want.

This book is broken down into three main sections. First, I'm going to bust show business myths. Yes, I mean those statements that everyone says, but not everyone can prove. Such as, "You have to move to NY to make it in theatre!" or "You have to get an agent and a manager to get decent work!" Everything in this business is relative. I'll share with you some stories (and secrets) from my time working in entertainment as well as stories from other colleagues of mine, whose credits span from Broadway and film to working with chart-topping musical acts.

The second part of this book is to give you a change of perspective. I'm going to delve into the mindset you have to operate from, in order for this guide to be effective for you. It's so much more than quick tips like "make sure you have clean sheet music to give to the piano player" or what performers can deduct from their taxes. This section will be a complete overhaul of how you confront your everyday problems and routines, using techniques that were used and perfected by the likes of Rockefeller and Carnegie. This part of the book is going to show you how to make opportunities fall in your lap simply by re-evaluating how you see yourself and the world around you.

The third part of this book is focused on giving you helpful insights and advice on everyday matters of people in show business, but through the point of view outlined in Section Two. I'll give you insight about marketing, agents, managers, unions, networking, training, taxes, and a slew of other topics to help you get the most of your career. I'm not going to sugarcoat any of it. It will be pragmatic. It will be ruthless. It will be effective. More effective than you would have ever dreamed before.

Consider this your first step in becoming exactly what you want to be and on your terms. Take this advice to heart, on both a professional and personal level. It's going to open doors for you that you never knew even existed.

Now that I've laid out the roadmap on how we're going to tackle this, let's get about the business.

SECTION ONE

Working Artist, Starving Artist

The New Business of Show Business

MYTH BUSTING

"Beware of false knowledge; it is more dangerous than ignorance."

- George Bernard Shaw

I n this business, you hear a lot of things. Some of them true, most of them not. The interesting thing is, unless you have a decent amount of experience, you don't know which is which. Some of these myths can cost you thousands of dollars and years of your life, when instead you could be making serious strides in your career. These myths are normally perpetuated by college professors who have been out of the field for years, other actors using the same failed techniques as the ones before them, and novices who only repeat what they've heard and have no experience to back up their opinions. We're going to bust some of the biggest myths right now.

1. You Have To Move To NYC Or LA In Order To Work In Entertainment

This is the biggest myth of all. There are opportunities literally everywhere you go. You just have to go and look for them. I'm a big believer… in order for you to be truly happy, you must first be happy where you are geographically. If you move to either NYC or LA, do it because you want to actually live there, not because you think the "best" opportunities are there. There are countless people that move to these cities with the idea of pursuing acting or something adjacent and end up burning out because they don't actually like living there.

The other factor to think about when moving to one of these cities is the cost of living. NYC and LA have some of the most expensive real estate in the world and the cost of living is exponentially higher than the majority of the country. A lot of times people get to these cities with the best of intentions of pursuing a career in entertainment and wind up becoming career waitresses, caterers, store clerks, etc., just to pay the rent. They find that they put their dreams of making it in entertainment to the side in order to live. That doesn't sound like fun, does it?

I am, by no means, anti-New York or LA, but I am anti-"winging it". Those that are truly successful have a set plan of how to make it happen. It's slow, it's steady, and it's measureable. So when looking for jobs, look outside the box. For example, when I first started in this business, I started out by living in the basement of my friend's house in Raleigh, NC. This was before I had any plan of action, let alone any idea on how to start. So I started to read and do lots of research about people I would like to emulate. I also started studying marketing and business techniques, which no one ever taught me in school. After a few months, I started to formulate a plan on what I wanted and how I intended to get it. I then used several marketing strategies (which I will discuss later in the book) to look for jobs all over the U.S. I had little to no experience on my résumé, besides some small professional summer work I had done in college. I landed a job as the Assistant Music Director for the number one, highest rated Amusement Park in the world. From there, I switched to become their Lead Music Director. I then landed a job as a Music Director for a major cruise line. Literally, within three months, I went from living in my friend's basement to music directing in the Virgin Islands. The next year, I led a group in opening for two major Top 40 recording artists. There are opportunities everywhere to get you to "the next step," you just have to know how to look for it.

I tell you this story not to show my career path, but the resources it has given me. Within that one year, I had paid off all my debt (student loans and otherwise) and had enough resources to go anywhere in the country and live comfortably. From that point on, I could choose what job offers I wanted to take and live on my own terms. No temp jobs. No scraping the couch for change to pay rent. It was a plan and it was a process, all of which I'll cover in later sections of this book.

2. You Don't Need To Go To School To Go Into This Business

Now, this statement is theoretically true. However, the statement itself has a very narrow look at this business. It's true that you don't have to go to school to get into this business, but it can definitely separate the amateurs from the professionals.

From a Music Director's point of view, you can easily tell who has been trained in audition techniques, vocal pedagogy, and presentation. It's a discipline that you can only learn from taking classes on the subject and years of practice. It's an ever-evolving art form and you need to keep learning to make yourself better, which requires discipline.

I have one prime example of how the discipline speaks volumes above anything else. I knew a man who was the Dean of a very successful theatre program, and he preached discipline above all things. He knew that persistence was going to get you ahead. His background is a bit different from what you would expect from a typical professor of theatre. Yes, he had lots of great Broadway and TV/Film credits and had been on a number of syndicated shows. However, before jumping into the entertainment business, he ran a military prison for prisoners-of-war in Vietnam as an enlisted officer. That's just about as serious as it gets. This professor instilled every one of his students with the discipline and respect you would expect from someone in that position. You knew your material, you were never late, and you were always present and attentive. Let me tell you, it shows in the work. Once I started directing for bigger entertainment companies and we would audition at this school, they cast more people from there than any other audition combined. Why? Because their discipline showed and it put them in high demand. Many of the same students now work year-round, doing exactly what they went to school for. Get the training; it's worth the investment.

3. If You Are Successful In School, You'll Be Successful In The Real World

It seems contradictory, but it's a trap lots of people fall into. We all know the type, the professors' favorites, and the ones that get the lead in every main stage show. It's a great opportunity, but not one to predict your future. Remember, everything you do at school is only relative to that school.

One of the biggest things you need to do is consider the source. What is the background of your professors? What is the last professional job they held (other than teaching)? Why did they decide to teach, instead of still working in the field? These are all important questions to ask to make sure you are getting the most up-to-date information and the best training. If your professor's last gig was the early 80's, you can pretty much bet a good amount of the information you're getting about the business side of this industry is outdated. When your professors tell you that in the "real world" you need to always have two Shakespearean and two contemporary monologues that you will use for every audition, you can bet that is a bit of a stretch. Not to say you shouldn't have material prepared, but just because you have four great monologues doesn't mean you're going to use them for everything you go in for. If they tell you that you need to wear a button down and a tie to an audition, or that the girls should wear those bright-colored dresses with nude pumps, you can cool believe that's an outdated practice. Of course, you need to look presentable at auditions, but if you dress like you're going to church, that's the first thing to give it away, you're new to the business.

Once again, you need to consider the source. If you want to learn how to be rich, do you talk to someone who makes $30 thousand a year or a millionaire? The answer is obvious. The same rule applies to learning this business. Talk to people working in the field, you'll learn more from them about the business than out-dated professors. This is not to say that the actual training your professors give you, apart from the business aspect, is outdated. The instruction on how to play scales on an instrument or how to analyze a scene is the same pretty much wherever you go, so that training is great to have. What I'm saying here is be mindful of the advice you receive about the business side of the entertainment industry. You want to have the most up-to-date information as possible.

Another factor, always be cognizant that you're prioritizing what you are learning, and it might not necessarily be directly related to the arts. With the advent of YouTube and Facebook, how we find jobs and how we are marketed is totally different than what it was even five years ago. So take classes in marketing and business, because in order to survive show business, you need a good mix of both. Sadly, talent only accounts for a fraction of this business; the rest is how you sell yourself. Just remember, it's called best-selling author and not best-writing author for a reason!

4. If You Are Meant To Be A Star, You Will Be One

Success is something you define and find for yourself; fame is given to you. Know the difference. I hear people say all the time that they want to be famous, all the while not realizing that fame is not a solid goal. Fame is a fleeting illusion. It's not measureable, and it's not obtainable by itself.

However, success is a vision you have for yourself, accomplished through goals that are set by you. If you are focused on what you want, with a very clear vision and with discipline, you will find success. Once that happens, people will begin to take notice as a by-product.

One of my favorite stories in regard to this is singer/ songwriter, Jimmy Buffett (of Margaritaville fame). He's a great example of sticking to what you believe in and pursuing your idea of success no matter what that entails. He's on record saying that the only reason he started a band was to "get free drinks and pick up chicks."[1] He played in bars in Louisiana and even had a stint in Nashville. When he was trying to get a record deal, he was repeatedly turned down because his music didn't fit into a specific category. He wasn't quite country, and he wasn't quite reggae or anything in between. However, he continued to play and tour around and eventually he wrote Margaritaville and his career took off. He then opened a chain of restaurants, casinos, and hotels. Too this day, he's still one of the highest grossing touring acts in the country. That was his idea of success and he pursued it all the way to fruition. During a TV interview he said, "It's kind of ironic to me that I was never catagorizable and now I'm a category."[1] That's about as clear-cut an example you can get. You have to know exactly what you want, otherwise, you'll be lost trying to find the unobtainable.

5. You Have To Have An Agent And/Or Manager

You see it all the time, people that just start in this business then rush to find an agent and a manager. They spend lots of time researching and taking classes, hoping they can get into some sort of agency. They eventually get signed with an agent/ manager, and it becomes a lot of hurry up and wait. They don't get sent out that often or they get sent out for the wrong things because their agent is asleep at the wheel. It seems a bit counter-productive.

Yes, for big budget productions, it's much easier to be seen if you have an agent, but at what cost? Years of struggling, hoping to find the "big break?" Or would it make more sense to take matters in your own hands and build yourself up? This way you can work consistently, building up your résumé and connections, to the point where you HAVE to have an agent and a manager to help manage your career.

You'd be surprised what types of gigs you can land without the help of either. It just takes time and research. I've known people to book decent regional and national commercials, national tours, and mid-high level budget movies. Solely, because they built themselves up to that level, and once they got to that level, they had agents and managers calling them and placing bids. I'll get more into how to do this in Section Three of this book.

Agents and managers are tricky; you have to get them at the right time in your career and under the right circumstances. Also keep in mind, when you are first starting out, you won't be getting the million dollar contracts. You'll be getting offers that are substantially smaller than that, and you'll have to budget what money you do get to be able to keep going in this business and not burn out. Your manager will take 15% of the total of what you earn, the agent 10%, plus add in taxes around 15% and living expenses/bills, you have quickly dwindled down your paycheck. It's all about the timing and where you are in your career, both professionally and financially, that will determine how effective an agent and manager will be for you.

A fun story to finish off this myth, and little known fact, actor Bill Murray does not have an agent. All the movies he has starred in were on his own accord. He has an 800 hotline people can call and pitch movies to him. And when he makes a movie deal, it's a "gentlemen's agreement" and you just hope he shows up at the studio on the first day of filming[2].

I'm by no means telling you to open a hotline and let people pitch projects to you, but what I am saying is you can cover a lot of ground in this business by yourself and with your own good sense. You just have to be disciplined enough to go for it.

6. You Have To Pay For Connections

One of the biggest traps I see people fall into is believing they have to pay elaborate amounts of money for master classes and professional development courses in order to make connections. I hear stories all the time about new people coming to this business and getting advice from other performers who have been working in places like NYC or LA, but haven't gotten any further in their career than someone just starting out. It goes back to what I said earlier, do you want to learn how to become rich from someone who makes 30 thousand a year or a millionaire?

Two things to keep in mind about any class you sign up for; 1) Are you taking this class for the right reason (i.e. you actually want/need to learn what's being taught), and 2) Does the person teaching it really have your best interest in mind? Many times performers will sign up and pay a decent amount of money for classes with a "big name casting agent" or "new and acclaimed director." After it's done, they feel very underwhelmed, because they received no individual attention and they wasted their money. Why do you think this is? Because more often than not, these people are teaching classes just to line their pockets to help offset their living costs. Odds are, the only reason these casting directors/agents/directors are able to pursue what they are doing is because you are paying them to do that. They may not know any more than you do, other than how to take money out of your pocket and put it in theirs.

Now, this is not to say there aren't good courses to take. You just need to be able to deliberate and filter through the bad ones. A good tip to help with this is not only do research of who is teaching the class but who has taken the class. Ask your friends and colleagues about the same class and see what they are doing now. If they are finding consistent success, the class is probably a safe bet. You should also look at the price point for the class and the amount of people taking it. If they are asking for a great amount of money, yet they haven't rented a studio for the class, that should put up a red flag. If the class is more than 15 people, you probably won't be getting any individual attention, which is what you are paying the money for in the first place. This boils down to discipline and research. You must pay your due diligence to make sure you are getting exactly what you pay for.

7. You Can't Make Money In This Business

This statement, I believe, is the most common myth you hear about show business. I also believe it's the most incorrect one. Money is everywhere; you just need to know how and where to look.

Years ago, it used to be easier to move to a big city with minimal resources, limited connections, and self-motivation to make a living. Today, the stakes are a bit higher. Due to increasing living costs, taxes, inflation, and an over-saturation of people, it's significantly harder to pursue a career in the arts without the proper resources and planning. You must have a financial stronghold in order to give yourself the freedom to go to auditions whenever needed, and move for a gig when necessary.

One of the biggest downfalls of the school system, I believe, is the lack of financial education, and without a good foundation to stand on, it's easy to let your financial stability start to slip. This is especially true for working artists because of how sporadic work, i.e. a paycheck, can be. So the best way to survive in show business is to have some sense about business, and that's exactly what this book is aiming to address. When you have a strong business and financial foundation, your stress about where your next paycheck is coming from is completely vanished. You can be more selective about what jobs you take, and more importantly, you can spend more time building yourself and your business.

The name of the game is not how much money you make, but how much money you keep. The more money you keep, the longer you can live off of it. It sounds like an oxymoron but you don't realize how much money is spent on classes, agents, unions, headshots, promotional materials, and living expenses until you find ways to drastically reduce or cut it out of your budget. For example, many non-union tours, with the same production value and schedules as union tours, are paying the same amount as union tours, except you don't have to give a cut to your agent, manager, or union. That's not only a great thing to have on your résumé; it's also smart business.

Just keep in mind; the amount of money you make is directly proportionate to how well you know yourself and how well you sell yourself. Anything else is just icing on the top. I will discuss this in much greater depth later in the book.

8. You Have To Pay Your Dues

Now, before you think I'm a crazy person saying you don't have to put your work in, think about this. If you know exactly what you want and exactly where you are going, the path (and the jobs) you take will become much clearer to you. Many actors go out and try to make a name for themselves. They end up working in the costume shop of the theatre, or they end up working at the box office and write it off as "I'm just paying my dues." They find themselves not on stage very often, but more so doing the job that is "paying their dues." Something about this seems wrong. Yes, you have to build up a name for yourself, but not at the expense of doing what you set out to do. All too often performers, designers, directors, everyone in this business get pulled away from what they are trying to go after, often under the illusion they are paying their dues to get them closer to what they want. Not realizing they are prolonging the achievement of their dream.

The best example of this is of a violinist I knew who had graduated with his Masters in Music. He didn't want to go back to school to get his Doctorates and teach, but he actually wanted to go out and make a living as a musician. He had played in certain symphonies during school but never for anything of prominence. However, his goal was to be first chair for a major symphony orchestra. And he applied for dozens and dozens of symphonies, and was offered several jobs because of his excellent musicianship; but none of them were for first chair. The excuses he always got was, "You have to work your way up to first chair." And he has seen enough in this business to know that people will go 20+ years going for first chair, and never get it because of politics or some other outside reasons. So he was determined to step into a symphony starting as first chair and nothing less. It took him three years. He didn't take another music job until he got exactly what he wanted, because every "no" he heard just fueled him even more to keep going.

If you know the end goal, then that's exactly what you have to go for. If you settle for fifth or sixth chair in hopes you might get moved up to first, then you have already sold yourself short. Go for the gold and be crazy enough to ask for it, because those are the ones who get exactly what they want. The only dues you have to pay are the ones you make for yourself. So, why not go for broke? You can fail just as easily at something you don't want to do, so why not risk it for something you really want?

SECTION TWO

Working Artist, Starving Artist

The New Business of Show Business

THE PERSPECTIVE

"The only thing standing between you and your dreams is the bullshit story you keep telling yourself that you can't."

– Jordan Belfort

I know this industry goes by the name "show business," but in reality the word business should come first. In order to survive in this industry, you have to have some sense of business. In order to have a good sense of business, you need to change your way of thinking, and that's exactly what this section is about. Even though you are artistically minded, you must also be business minded; which is almost a contradiction in terms. If you tap into your true artistic ability while simultaneously changing your view and learning how business actually works, you will truly be limitless in what you can achieve.

One of the biggest problems I see most often is witnessing professionals of all levels (both beginners and seasoned professionals) getting caught up in the excitement of a company wanting them in their production, but neglecting to figure out the means at which they need to survive. They take menial amounts of money, sometimes have to pay exorbitant amounts of money for short-term housing, no travel included, and realize after taxes and any other fees (such as agents/managers/unions/ etc.) they have saved no money and often times, leave with less money than they started with. Instead, you need to think of a way to thrive in your personal life in conjunction with being successful in the business of show.

The key rule to life is that you have to set a premium for yourself. People value you as much as your value yourself. Really think about that. If you think you are worth $12 an hour, then your boss will believe that's all you're worth and maybe less. If you set the standard for yourself, then why wouldn't you set it much higher? Something you know you are truly worth. Why not $15 an hour? $300 a day? $3,000 a week? $10,000 a week? All of that is truly attainable. You just have to set the premium for yourself and find the way to get there. That's what this section is really about, which is getting you in the right frame of mind in order to achieve success you thought would never be within your reach.

1. Don't Tell Me What I Can't Do!

The first thing you need to do is decide exactly what it is that you want. You have to be very specific here. Much like acting or designing, specificity is key. If you don't know exactly where you want to end up, you will never get there. Much like asking for directions to someone's house and all they tell you is the city they live in. It's not very useful if you don't have the specific address. Otherwise, you'll be wandering around a city you don't know all day. The same thing applies for life and career goals. The difference: instead of one day, you'll be wondering the rest of your life. You have to be very clear as to what it is that you want and set goals and benchmarks to reach them. For example, moving to New York and "try acting" is not a good goal. It's a statement. A good example of a goal would be, " I want to be a supporting character in a new Broadway musical written by Mel Brooks, directed by Susan Stroman, within the next three years." It's a good goal because it's specific. It's clear in its intention and has a clear timeline of when it needs to be accomplished.

So how do you meet the three-year limit? That's where the thinking comes in. If you just said that you were moving to New York and "try acting," there is no goal in which to build a plan. However, when you start adding specifics, the path becomes clearer. How do I get in front of Susan Stroman? How do I get to sit down and meet Mel Brooks? Who is casting the show? Who is producing the show? Who do I know that's associated with any of them? Are they part of any regional theatres? Can I get to one of them?

Do you see where I'm going with this? Because you added specifics, you can now find ways to reach that goal. You might be able to work with the producers that Mel Brooks and Susan Stroman have worked with in the past. You might be able to work with them in some capacity, such as, a workshop setting outside of New York. If you have friends that have worked with them, find a way to get introduced. You'll be surprised how quickly things can happen when you have a specific goal and aren't afraid to ask.

A great example of the power of specificity is the great, late-night talk show host, Johnny Carson. When he first moved to L.A. to pursue his dream, he didn't say, "I'm going to L.A. to pursue comedy". He had a master plan. He had three, time-sensitive goals. His first goal was within one year be a head writer for a TV show on a network station. So he started a very low-budget sketch comedy show on KNXT, a local L.A. television station. Because he took the leap and put himself out there, Red Skelton saw the show and asked him to join his writing team for his nationally syndicated show. Goal one accomplished.

His second goal was to be a guest star of a national TV comedy show within two years. Because of his success on Red Skelton, he was asked to appear on the Jack Benny show, another successful show along the lines of Red Skelton, and sometimes even filled in for Red Skelton. Goal two accomplished.

The third goal was to be the host of his own show within three years. Well, because of his success with Jack Benny and Red Skelton (among others), CBS asked him to do the Johnny Carson show, which he did for two years. And then after that gig, he landed The Tonight Show. As they say, the rest is history.[3]

So how did he accomplish all of this? He had specific, time-sensitive goals and he was disciplined enough to stick to the plan. It's just that simple.

The next thing you need to understand is yourself. I know that sounds cliché but people forget how powerful that statement is. You must truly understand how you work and how you respond to problems and issues when they arise.

So, before you do anything, you need to discover what your mental boundaries are. By boundaries, I don't mean things such as "I will never do cocaine." I'm talking about boundaries that you might not even realize you have, mental boundaries that are established by your environment that you are not even aware of. A good example of this would be, "get a good education and a safe secure job." Odds are if you are reading this book, you've already broken through this particular boundary, because there is no such thing as "secure" when it comes to entertainment work. However, you can make your own personal life and finances secure if you choose to look at the world from another perspective. This is why I say you must discover your mental boundaries. When you can't afford rent and acting isn't paying the bills, do you quit? Absolutely not! You find another way. Maybe move somewhere cheaper where you can still perform and do what you love, while building up financial stability so you can afford where you want to live. Finding a temp job isn't the solution, because you end up doing work that doesn't feed you mentally/spiritually/financially. You take temp jobs to survive. I see it time and time again where people get stuck into temp jobs and loose sight of what they were going for in the first place. They didn't make a specific plan, they just went up with high hopes and dreams, but even dreams are useless without a plan of action.

Remember when I was discussing high-priced classes and workshops in the last section? Essentially when you are spending money on these classes, you are fulfilling someone else's dream. You are paying these people so that they can fulfill their dream of being a casting director/director/designer/etc.

Now see it from another way. Why can't you do the same? I was an actor/musician who learned how to play the piano and was getting no acting work. So, I asked myself how I could use my talents another way and still be in the same realm of what I want to do. I started teaching acting and vocal lessons to graduating college kids. After a while, because my students would put my name on their résumés and would tell others I was their teacher, I started to gain a foothold. From there, I was able to perform and play the piano, eventually building my way up to becoming a Music Director. All of a sudden, I didn't need to teach lessons anymore. I was working solely as a director and performer when I wanted.

You can apply this same principle to yourself. Think of other ways to build up your reputation and don't do what everyone else is doing. Find a way to fund your dream. Find different ways to use your talent to get to where you want to be. It's a lot like being in a maze. You try all the different possibilities. Trying to find the way out and by process of elimination, you eventually find the way that works.

One of the most influential books I've ever read (and you should read it immediately after putting this book down) is, *Think and Grow Rich* by Napoleon Hill. The book is centered on the successes of John D. Rockefeller and Andrew Carnegie and their perception of how they obtained wealth and success.[4]

The book suggests that you must list what you want out of life, where you want to be, and under what circumstances you want to live. And be very specific about all of it. So if you say you want a beach house in Florida, don't just say that. Describe the house, all the way down to the color of the carpet. Because once you write it down, it becomes something real and tangible.

After you have written all these things down, read it every night before bed and every morning when you wake up. Commit it to memory.

Essentially what you are doing here is training your subconscious with positive, productive thoughts. Your everyday movement and actions are controlled by your subconscious. If you train your subconscious to make actions that push you to your goal, you will be making steps to success without even realizing it.

Think of it this way, why are people afraid of snakes? Most of the time, these people have never had an altercation with one, so why are they afraid of them? It's because their subconscious has been fed negative thoughts of interacting with them over the years, via other people's interactions or some other type of input. So, if you can feed your subconscious to have a visceral negative reaction to something that is *perceived* as bad, why can't the opposite be true?

If you feed your mind with positive and specific goals, then you will subconsciously make every decision and action to accomplish these goals. Make a plan and stick with it.

2. Failure Is Not A Step Back, It's A Step Forward

One of my favorite stories is that of treasure hunter, Mel Fisher. Mel Fisher is famous for discovering the 1622 wreck of the Spanish galleon Nuestra Señora de Atocha and its famous treasure cache known as "The Atocha Motherlode." This treasure included over $450 million in gold, silver, and emeralds. He searched for this treasure for over 15 years. He had to keep his crew motivated, so every morning he would proclaim, "Today is the day!" He said it everyday for 15 years. One day they actually found the Atocha thus fulfilling his self-made prophecy of "today is the day!"[5] To put it a bit more plainly, "You can quit at any time, so why quit now?"[6] If Mel had quit one day, he would have never found his treasure.

The same principle applies to your career and your path to success. If you feel like nothing is happening for you, don't blame it on the world or anyone else. Instead, look inwards and figure out why something isn't clicking for you. Just remember, there is always another way. If you can't get through the front door, try to find a way into the side door. If there isn't a side door, try climbing through a window. You have to constantly re-evaluate how you pursue your goals. You have to ask yourself, "Is there a better way to do this?" If you are doing what the majority of everyone else is doing, you're probably doing it wrong. You're working hard, not smart.

If Mel hadn't constantly re-evaluated how he was searching for his treasure, he would have never found it. If he only searched for five miles using radar that only went 400 feet down, he never wound have found the wreck that was 12 miles out and 600 feet deep. He constantly expanded where he thought it could be and critiqued the method he used to find it, until eventually he struck gold. He never lost sight of what he was after, but he refined his method until it worked. So were the 15 years beforehand a failure? Absolutely not. They were one step closer to success. Instead of considering mistakes as "failures," switch the word "failure" with "experiment." When you do experiments, it implies you are trying something new and that every setback you have is an opportunity to learn how to make the next experiment better. Therefore, failure is not a step back; it's a step forward.

One of the best ways to find alternate roads to success is to see what everyone else is doing and do the opposite. It forces you to think and re-evaluate why things are done a certain way and to help you come up with a better plan.

Think about it this way. Have you ever been through the drive-thru at McDonald's and there were 12 cars in line but look inside and realize there was no one in there? So, what do you do? Do you stay in the drive-thru line and wait 30 minutes? NO! You park your car, get out and order, and get back in your car in five minutes. You just saved 25 minutes and you have your food before everyone else. Why? Because you saw what everyone else was doing and did the complete opposite.

If you think of auditions and making connections the same way, you'll find new and innovative ways of reaching your goals through both failure and success. You just have to stick to the plan and never loose sight of where you are heading.

3. There's No People Like Show People

Show people are some of the most open and friendly people you will ever meet. But one fact is true, no matter what business you are in, people often put on a "show". They aren't really interested in you. They're just interested in what you can offer them. Show people are just the best at hiding their intentions.

I say this not to ruffle feathers, but to point out something a lot of people fail to recognize. 98% of people in the world ask the question, "what can you give to me?" The most *successful* people in the world ask the question, "what can I give to you?" Understand, however, when you ask the second question, it benefits both parties. Here's an example why.

Imagine people have an imaginary sign around their neck that says, "Make me feel good." Everyone loves talking about themselves, and letting others talk about themselves makes them feel good. If you make someone feel good, they will remember you and very likely help you with whatever you need.

Think about this. Most people go into an audition or a job interview asking for a job. This is a bad way to look at it. Instead of asking for something, think about what you can give them. Your job is to help find a solution to their problem. So, take the focus off of you and put it on them. I know this sounds counterintuitive to what you have been taught to do, but remember, you don't want to do what everyone else is doing.

So talk to them like regular people, because that's what they are. They are no more important or better than you are. You'll quickly find out when you look at auditions and interviews with this point of view, your opportunities will increase tenfold. Remember, everyone wants to be in the spotlight one way or another, so why not try being the operator for a change and put yourself in control of the situation? I'll discuss this more in-depth in Section Three.

A good friend of mine used this tactic to his advantage a couple of years ago. He was working on a modernized jazz revue to sell to presenting agencies and hopefully tour the country with it. Well, in order to get footage and a foundation to start with, he needed to find a theatre to produce it.

He came across this new start-up theatre on the central coast of California that was producing newer and modern plays. He decided he would volunteer his time at this theatre and build a relationship with them. He knew this theatre was a start-up and was always looking for new sources to profit from. So he pitched his jazz show to them, with the caveat that he would do it for free but split whatever the box office made and all refreshment profits would go to the theatre. The theatre, of course, agreed. My friend created a situation that was advantageous to everyone involved. And because he volunteered his time and self-produced his own show, he was able to properly market and sell his jazz revue to venues across the country.

It sounds like a cliché piece of advice but it still holds true, if you know what you are going after in life and are selfless in how you treat people, the opportunities you seek will present themselves to you.

4. Always Expand Your Horizons

One of the most dangerous things you can do, and it happens all to often, is to become comfortable; comfortable with your skills, your living situation, your career, your personal life, anything that affects you on a daily basis. In order to really grow as a person and in your career, you constantly need to expand your horizons. You must constantly stretch yourself beyond what you think you are capable of.

Remember, you are a product of your environment and you are in complete control of what environment you are in. You have to make sure that you are surrounding yourself with positive and progressive people because negativity will kill creativity.

One of my favorite speakers and motivators, Tai Lopez, presented a Ted Talk about how to grow as a person. In his speech, he explained the law of 33%. The law of 33% is a guideline to help you control your environment and in turn help you grow as a person. The basis of the rule is you need to spend 33% of your time with people that are below your current level. You can mentor them (especially after reading this book) and they in turn will make you feel good for helping them and give you more motivation to keep going upwards.

The next step is you need to spend 33% of your time with people on the same level as you. These people become your friends and your peers and you help each other get to the next level.

And the last step is to spend 33% of your time with people that are 10-20 years ahead of you. This way, you aren't being lead by someone who only has marginal success, but someone who has proof of what they have accomplished in the next level. So if you want to start a million dollar company, you need to find someone who has a ten million dollar company to mentor you.

Talking and hanging out with the 33% above your level should make you feel uncomfortable, but that's a great thing. It means you are growing. You have to constantly push beyond yourself.[7]

Don't forget, who you hang out with is a direct reflection of you. So it's your job to evaluate the professional and personal habits of the people you hang out with and see how you compare. What do you see? What do they do when they make money? Do they spend it all on useless items? Do they go out every night and blow it on drinking? Do they sit on the couch all day and smoke it? Or do they save and re-invest what they make? Do they study to learn how to become better spenders and people?

Once again, you are a reflection of your actions and your environment. If you want to become a millionaire, or a famous actor, or successful director, you must emulate those that already are. As Bruce Lee once said, "Long-term consistency outdoes short-term intensity."[8] You are affected by your environment, so make sure that it is pushing you to where you want to go.

So one of the most important things you can do for yourself and your career is to get rid of any negativity in your life. Any bad habits you see in other people, look within yourself and make sure you aren't making the same mistakes. Constantly evaluate yourself to make sure you are doing everything in your power to get to a point of homeostasis; a point where your passion, your goals, your environment, and your thoughts and actions are all pushing you towards your ultimate goal. Once you have reached this point, opportunities will begin to present themselves.

SECTION THREE

Working Artist, Starving Artist

The New Business of Show Business

THE BUSINESS

"How can you squander even one more day not taking advantage of the greatest shifts of our generation? How dare you settle for less when the world has made it so easy for you to be remarkable?"

- Seth Godin

The main purpose of this book is to give you a different point of view about show business. The reason this book is structured in three main sections is simple.

The first section, Busting Show Business Myths, was to show you "conventional" wisdom about this business and how many things you were told were hard and true facts are, in reality, not so truthful. I wanted to show there was another side to the coin that most people fail to see and that everything is relative.

The next section, The Perspective, was to give you the tools to be able to think differently about success and motivation, and hopefully give you a better point of view on this business. The point of view that few people ever get to experience, because they follow the crowd and never stop to think, "Wait. Maybe there's a better way to do this."

All of that leads me to this section, The Business. This section is here to give you advice and insight on a laundry list of topics pertinent to this field. However, I'm giving advice from the point of view of the successful 2% and not the other 98% of people aimlessly doing what everyone else is doing. I'm talking to you from the point of view of someone who uses the rules and advice from Section Two to make the business work for them, not the other way around.

I'm going to break down this section into two sub-sections. The first half will be focused more on the artistic side of the business and the pros and cons of the types of work available to you. The second half, "Know Your Market," will focus on the business aspects of the entertainment industry and how to make this business work for you.

Some of this advice may be controversial to you. It may go against everything you have been taught or have heard previous to this. But remember no one ever got ahead by doing what everyone else was doing. I want this section to stretch how you see every aspect of this business and hopefully open a door for you. I want you to be able to see this business for what it really is and make it work for you.

I will set this section up like a reference guide and the topics will be as follows:

- Auditions

- Audition Conventions

- Internships

- Cruise Ships and Theme Parks
- Children's Theatre
- Regional/Dinner Theatres
- National Touring
- Graduate School
- Workshops and Masterclasses
- Know Your Market
- Webpage and Promotions
- Networking
- Agents and Managers
- Unions
- Negotiating and Contracts
- Financial Planning
- Taxes
- Your Day Job

AUDITIONS

"The Human Element"

Auditions are the cornerstone to getting a job as a performer. It's the most common practice in the entire industry. Everyone talks about it and everyone has a different view on what the most successful method is. However, no one really talks about the truth of an audition, the one undeniable fact that everyone forgets; the human element of the audition.

Yes, you are auditioning for a certain role/character/ singer/ etc. but more importantly; they are also looking at you as a person. Even if on a subconscious level, people are attracted (and more willing to hire) people that are compatible with them as a person. So, your goal is to put yourself mentally on the same level as those in charge.

All too often, people see casting directors and anyone else "above them" as better than they are. That's a debilitating way to think. That mindset puts you at the mercy of those hiring, as opposed to putting yourself in a situation with power and control. Remember, you're dealing with *people* and every casting director/director/designer/etc. puts their pants on one leg at a time just like you do. If you see yourself as equals with them, you will get a better response from every audition and interview you do.

"Well-executed Simplicity"

The best thing you can do at an audition is what you do well. If you are a belter, then belt. If you can riff, show them you can riff. If you aren't a belter, don't try to belt. And if you can't riff, make certain you don't riff.

You should have two or three go-to audition songs that are practiced to perfection. And make sure you pick songs that really work for your voice, character type, and style. It happens all too often that performers pick songs that are *just* under their range, or songs they like singing but don't really fit their type, or a style they have no business singing (like a jazz singer singing 80's rock).

Your best bet is to look for material that you understand on all levels. And look for material that not a lot of people are going to find. Some of the best places to find great songs are from musical flops. You really should take some time and study flops and find untapped material, because often times they have great audition songs. The best part of using untapped material is that it also becomes a talking piece. If you nail the song and really sell it, odds are they are going to ask you where it's from, and the more you get to talk to them the better.

"Be Different"

Oddly enough, most actors are afraid to take risks. That seems almost counter-intuitive to this industry, and a risk within itself. As I mentioned earlier, one of my key philosophies on life is to find out what everyone else is doing and do the opposite. Now this doesn't mean take arbitrary risks, but calculated and justifiable risks. Maybe sing a song from a different gender or a take on a scene that isn't performed as the stage directions read. Most of the time, especially with a new show, the director/writers want to see what you bring to the table, not if you can take what is prescribed to you.

A good friend of mine, Marissa, is a good example of this. She was auditioning for a new play and the role she was going in for was an OCD teenager with separation anxiety that just had her heart broken for the third time. She knew this type of audition was risky because it's easy to play the "mood" of the scene and she noticed that's what most people were doing. At that moment, she had an epiphany. In her bag, from the night before, she won this stuffed Rastafarian banana (you know, a smiling banana with dreads and the Jamaican hat). She immediately thought about Linus and his blanket from the Peanuts comics. What did he do when he became upset and anxious? He grabbed his blanket! So, she brought in the stuffed banana and cleaned off the chair and set the banana upright in the chair and started her monologue. As the monologue went on, and she became more anxious, she went behind the chair and grabbed the stuffed banana and held it close to her. At the end of the monologue, at the emotional climax, she holds out the banana and yells, "I'll never let them tear my heart out again." Which in turn made the writers and director laugh.

At the end of the audition, they applauded her for taking a chance with the banana. It was justified, and it gave another point of view to the material. She ended up booking the gig because of that one inspired and justifiable risk.

So the moral of the story is this, don't be afraid to step outside of the box and try something different, because if you do it right, it will be noticed and that recognition will take you a long way.

"Listening Is Key"

You can teach someone how to act, sing, and dance, but you cannot teach someone how to listen. Listening is the most important thing you can ever learn. And not just listening but empathetic listening. Empathetic listening is the ability to hear someone else talk and be able to fully understand their point of view and feelings. This is the key to acting and also to everyday life.

Often times, after an audition, a director will ask you to do your material (or sometimes different material) again but with some adjustments. Many performers will hear the direction, but it goes in one ear and out the other and they perform just as they did the first go around. They hope the second go around is good enough. This is a horrible strategy because it looks like you either, a) don't understand the direction, or b) just don't listen.

If you are given a direction at an audition and don't understand it, there is absolutely no shame in asking for clarification. Don't do it again unless you understand the direction. Most people are scared to death to ask for clarification. If you actually ask for clarification, not only will it look like you actually care, but it will also make you feel better knowing you actually understand the direction. Just remember, the squeaky wheel gets the grease.

"Show Them You"

The most important thing you can do is show the people behind the table who you are as a person. That's always rule number one; it's about people.

Another good tip to remember, and this is especially true at audition conventions, is that an audition is you trying to sell yourself to a company. Callbacks are when the company is trying to sell themselves to you. They want to see if you work well with them and their "product" (whatever show they are doing at the time) and if they work well with you. Take that opportunity to show them who you really are, your work ethic, and that you are perfect for the job. It then becomes a two-way street and that's a great position to be in.

AUDITION CONVENTIONS

"Proactive Is Key"

Imagine this scenario. You're sitting in a lecture hall for a class and you are required to be there all day. They have a series of guest speakers lined up for the entire day and the lectures are all based around one topic, the history of rocks. You take this class because you are required to do so, but you have absolutely no interest in the history of rocks. It sounds like your own little circle of hell, doesn't it? No offense to those rock lovers in the world, but it does become monotonous.

This is exactly how the people at audition conventions and large cattle calls feel, such as UPTA, SETC, NETC, Straw Hats, etc. The only difference is they hear a thousand people do the same audition for three days, not just one. Talk about a migraine for everyone involved.

So you ask yourself, how do I stand out amongst a thousand people who are auditioning for people whose brains have been completely fried and spattered against the wall? I'll tell you. And the secret is being proactive. I've said it before and I'll say it again. The squeaky wheel gets the grease.

If I'm sitting in one of these long cattle call auditions, odds are I will not remember you from your audition alone. And even worse, if you're not in the first 30 people to go in, I'm probably not even paying attention anymore. The way to combat this is to find the companies you are interested in before you go and send them your materials.

Every audition convention has a website, and on that website they list which companies and theatres have gone in the past and plan on going that year. Even better, most of the conventions websites provide you with a link to each company's website, so you don't even have to bother googling the theatres! When you research these companies, you can see what shows they have lined up and other really helpful information that will help you pick your audition materials accordingly.

Most importantly, you can find information on the casting and artistic directors and their contact information. Make sure you send them an email around the first of the year with your materials and what you think you would be good at in their season. Many times theatres will use audition conventions to just finish casting their shows, as they have cast several roles from other locations. This way you get ahead of the curb before the actual audition conventions start in February and March.

If you're proactive and send these companies your materials, you make yourself more marketable and are essentially helping them solve a problem. The problem being whom they should hire to adequately fill their roles. All good business people know the key to success is coming up with a solution to a problem.

You'll often times find out that when you do this, they'll already give you a callback (a "preemptive" callback might be the better term) at the audition convention and on some occasions even give you a job offer. Send an additional email 2-3 weeks before the convention as a friendly reminder that you'll be there and what number you will be.

Essentially, what you have done here is create your own luck. Now I want you to imagine this scenario after you've done the recommended footwork. It's the middle of the day, 375 auditions in, and you're up next. You walk on stage and say "Tyler Smith, number 376." At that moment, all those sleepy people out in the audience sit up, pay attention, and are completely focused on you. Because once you said your name and number, they recognize it, they've already talked with you, and now they are going to give you their full attention. Even if you go up and do a mediocre job on your audition, they will still call you back because you've already built the anticipation yourself. A lot of times they'll forgive a botched audition and let you have another shot at it because you were so persistent in the beginning. That's what I mean when I say being proactive is key.

Thinking back to earlier in the book about being able to talk to people and selling yourself as a person, the same rules apply in callbacks. These companies know that every other company at that audition convention wants you, so be humble and gracious. Remember, an audition is when you sell yourself to a company. A callback is where the company sells themselves to you.

"Business Over The Bar"

Remember what I said earlier about how this is a business about people, and the more you know about people, the better. This is why it's important to do your research about companies and people you want to work for. When you have this information, you already know their background and you have something solid to hold a conversation with.

Imagine this scenario. You finish all your auditions that day, walk down the street into a restaurant, and you see a group of artistic directors at the bar. You decide to walk up to the bar and buy a few of them a beer (classy move, by the way). Not only can you introduce yourself, you can also talk about what you already know. They might have mutual friends with you, they might have gone to the same school or you could talk about people you know who have worked with them before and their experience (all good, of course). Keep the conversation about them, not about you, and be genuinely interested in what they have to say. This goes back to empathetic listening, really take in everything.

What you have done by this exchange is not only make new friends, but it shows them your work ethic, that you've done your research, and that you are an easy person to get along with. I promise you one thing, you'll be one of the few (if not the only one) who actually took the initiative to make a good impression.

I was once doing a show out on the central coast of California, where I randomly met an Artistic Director for a theatre on the other side of the state. After seeing our show, she invited us to have dinner with her. Of course, we obliged.

In our dressing rooms, right before going to dinner, I used my phone and googled everything I could possibly find about her and the theatre. This way when I went to dinner, it looked like I already knew who she was and what her theatre did. She was completely taken aback that I knew lots of people that had worked there before, some of the theatre's history, as well as some more professional aspects about her. By the end of the dinner, she offered me a contract to music direct a show at her theatre. I gained this opportunity because I did the research and used what information I knew to better get to know her. That's why a little bit of research pays dividends. Know who you are talking with and use that information to get to know more. Besides, it never hurts to make a new friend.

"Don't Get Blindsided"

A common mistake that performers make, especially those who are new to the field, is lack of understanding of the job they are offered and based on the emotional excitement of being offered the job, it is accepted right away. You have to take the emotion out of it and fully know what you are being asked when offered a job.

There are tons of great jobs in the entertainment field. There are also a lot of really bad jobs. It's your responsibility to be able to decipher between the two. A good example of this happened to a friend of mine a few summers back.

He went to UPTA's and was offered two gigs, both the same salary but completely different in terms. One job offer was for the lead singer/setup tech of a theme park show (I'll withhold the name of said theme park) and one was to be the lead character/ setup tech for a dinner theatre. Both jobs were really appealing to him and he could have taken either offer, but he knew he needed to do his due diligence. So after the jobs were offered to him, he asked around to see which of his friends had worked there before. A few friends had worked at both places and what he discovered quickly made the decision for him.

He learned that even though the theme park offered the same salary and housing, the housing was located in a high crime part of town. He also learned the hours you spent doing tech work far exceeded the time he would be on stage. All of his friends who had worked there also said they had tried to shortchange them on paychecks several weeks in a row.

In comparison, the dinner theatre had a reputation of being very good to their performers. He learned the tech hours were minimal; he would only have to assist with strike. He also found out they provided housing in a nice condo downtown and the rent he would have to pay would be minimal. Of course, he went with the dinner theatre offer.

So, if he had taken the job just from what he was offered, he could have easily chosen the theme park and been miserable because he didn't know what he was getting into. Luckily, he decided to pay his due diligence and made the better choice.

The moral of the story here is don't be afraid to ask specifics when offered a job and also cross-check it with people who have been there before. It will save you a bunch of heartache just from taking the time to research.

"Fun, Money, and Résumé"

The final point of this section is why you take a job in the first place. I was offered this piece of advice from a choreographer friend of mine. She said, "You take a job for 3 reasons: Fun, Money, and Résumé. And if you don't have at LEAST two of the three, don't take the job." I use this often and it works every time.

Too often people take a job based off of only one of these, mostly either just for money or just for résumé. If you take a job for only one reason, you will not have a good experience. You have to take a job because it feels right and it goes into your plan of where you want to be. Taking a job must provide a solution to the next step of your master plan, just like I discussed in Section Two.

If you apply this principle to every offer you have, you'll quickly and without regret (which is very important) pick the right job for you.

I'll discuss more about the business side of picking job offers later in the book.

INTERNSHIPS

"Sprinkle A Little Magic Dust On It"

I'll start off this point with the most advertised internship in the world, The Disney College Program.

The Disney College program is an internship, at its most stripped down core, that gets college students with four-year degrees to do minimum skill work for minimum wage. Now, don't take this like I'm knocking down the program. I'm just seeing this from a business point of view. I'm looking at this through the lens of the point of view I laid out in Section Two.

When you apply for this program, they tell you it looks great on a résumé, that it will help you move up in the company, that you'll get to meet lots of interesting people in your business and all sorts of stuff. Now, see it from their perspective. If you knew you owned a business and you had hundreds of jobs that needed to be filled, such as; parking attendants, ride operators, and food service, how would you fill those positions? You would try to find the most people in a concentrated area that needed jobs. Where better to look than college kids fresh out of school? Plus, if you have a name like Disney, people would kill to have that sort of "credibility."

Now, let me tell you the cold business truth about it. Remember, we are talking about minimum skill/minimum wage jobs here. They require no training, no skill, and no education. What Disney Parks have done is brilliant from a business prospective. They have figured out a way to get college-educated people to do a minimum wage job with the promise of advancement within the company. If you were Disney and you had the most educated person willing to do the most minimal tasks, would you move them from that position? Absolutely not! Disney has every desirable position filled with a waiting list a mile long for every job in creative and upper management. Why would they move the educated people out of their internship level jobs? They wouldn't because it's better having someone in those positions with education and experience than someone with neither.

The reason they can "get away" with it is simply because they are Disney. They say it's good to have a Fortune 500 company on your résumé. And it is, just not in a minimum skill position. Internships are nothing more than a concept created by companies to get cheap labor. This is especially true in the entertainment business. Entertainment internships are not like your white-collar type of internships in fields such as marketing or research, where you plan to be there the majority of your life. They are generated to create cheaper labor, because the price of sustaining entertainment is so high compared to other fields of work.

If you are in your earlier years of college, internships in the entertainment field may be great for you because gaining the experience is necessary in honing your craft. However, if you are in your later years of college or have already graduated, an internship will only make you regret the position you put yourself in.

"For 60 Cents a Day, You Can Support An Actor In Need!"

My friend, Josh, once took an internship right out of college at a mid-sized repertory theatre in Pennsylvania. They were doing *Hello Dolly!* that year with some B-list celebrity and a decent-sized cast. They told Josh things like, "You get work along side this big star!" and "If you do this internship, it will be a great way to get in with us!" Of course, being right out of college and new to this business, he took the bait.

How he describes the situation now is something quite different. He realized very quickly that he was supposed to do all the "undesirable" jobs and work the crazy hours no one else was willing to do. But it was okay, because he had housing and meals taken care of and was even paid $50 a week! (Please note the sarcasm in this sentence.)

Once he was in this position, he realized what he actually signed up for. He was doing 14-hour rehearsal days as an ensemble member, as well as, putting several late night hours in the scene shop, essentially exhausting himself. Now let's do the math here.

If he was paid $50 a week and he worked six days, that would equal $8.33 a day. So, if he worked 14 hours a day, that would equal 60 cents an hour. That's right. 60 CENTS AN HOUR. Tell me how can you pay your student loans, credit card bills, and cell phone bill on 60 cents a day? Not to mention, we haven't even taken out taxes yet! (Which we will get to later in the book!)

The only reason Josh was in that position was because he put himself in that position. Make sure you really know what you are getting into before you take any job, especially if you are even considering taking a job in an internship.

THEME PARKS/CRUISE SHIPS

"If They Say Six Shows, They Mean Six Shows."

Theme parks are a great way to start off in show business, especially if you are looking to pursue music. Theme parks give you certain performance opportunities that you could not traditionally get elsewhere, such as, *Stomp* style shows, large rock/pop type events, even more "out-of-the-box" type of entertainment such as *Riverdance*. Theme parks often pay decent starting salaries compared to other venues such as regional theatre and low-budget films. So, for someone who is starting out or needs a good short-term contract, theme parks are a great place to look.

However, when you take a job at a theme park, know what is stated in your contract and know what is expected of you. When your contract says you will do six 25-minute shows a day, they mean you will be doing six shows a day for six days a week. So, if you take a theme park job, be prepared to work.

Every theme park is different with the amount/length of their respective shows. Some theme parks only have three 40-minute shows a day and some even only have one big show a day, like *Fantasmic* at Disney World or *Luminosity* at Cedar Point. Just know what you are capable of and your limitations. If you feel like doing five shows a day is a bit much for you, try for a park that doesn't do as many shows.

Another important thing to note is that a lot of theme park shows are performed outside. Now, this might not be so bad if you are somewhere like Maine for the summer, but if you're in North Carolina or Florida it's a whole different story. Performing outside in the heat can be a very exhausting venture, especially if you have to do it several times a day. So make sure when you are offered a job, you know whether or not it's performed outside. Now if it's one show a day outside at night, it's not that taxing. But if it's several shows during the middle of the day, it's definitely something to consider.

For those that want to do theme park work, I've come to realize there is a fit for everyone; you just need to know your strengths. Too often people come into these contracts thinking they can do six shows a day and they just cannot handle it, either physically, emotionally, or both. And if you don't fulfill your contract obligations, that's a good way to get a bad reputation in this business, no matter if you want to stay in theme parks or branch out into other venues. So, that's why I say, if they say six shows a day, they mean six shows.

Read your contract. Know what you are getting into.

"20,000 Leagues Under The Sea"

You remember the story of Captain Nemo and the Nautilus. It's the novel by Jules Verne about how Captain Nemo explores the sea for corals, abandoned shipwrecks, and the city of Atlantis. It's all very intriguing and fantastical until they run into the unexpected. Something none of them saw coming. They were attacked by a pack of giant squids, thus crippling the submarine and killing a crew member.

Working on a cruise ship can often feel the same way. And no, I'm not implying you will get attacked by a pack of giant squids. What I am saying is, it's easy to get caught up in the romanticism of sailing the ocean and exploring the world while getting paid a decent amount of money to perform. That's like finding the Atlantis of the entertainment world! But, just like Captain Nemo, don't get blindsided with the treasure and not see what else is beneath the waves. I'm going to give you a little insight to help ward off any future giant squid attacks you might run into.

Cruise ships are a fantastic way to make money. If you're part of the production shows on any major cruise line, you're looking at three to four different 45-minute shows that are performed twice on performance days (an early seating and a late seating.) So if your itinerary has you on a seven-day cruise, you will theoretically work three days and have four days off, since they only put each show on once a cruise rotation. Not bad for $1,100 (the average salary between singers and dancers for cruise lines) a week, right? Ah, but there is more. We haven't talked about the giant squid yet.

Cruise lines are notorious for giving performers other contractually obligated duties that aren't negotiated (unless you know they are there!). These duties can range from tending to the ship library for a five-hour shift, helping disembark guests, or even stagehand duties. Even more than this, they will compile other "performance duties" around the ship, such as character breakfasts where you might be asked to dance with certain cartoon characters.

For instance, on Norwegian Cruise Lines at the time of this writing, they have a partnership with Nickelodeon for their kids program. Every other day there is a breakfast at 6:30 in the morning for the little kids to meet and dance with the costume characters and the production cast dancers are expected to go and "party" with the characters. These types of things often occur on your "day off," so in reality, you might not have an actual day off if you don't negotiate some of this stuff out of your contract. I even knew some people that were on a four-day, cruise-ship itinerary and never had a day off because they had three production shows. They were so busy they couldn't even get off the ship for their ports-of-call. They could only leave for a couple of hours in their home port of Miami to get some supplies and get back in time for the opening show. That's not a great way to live for six months.

Another thing you need to be aware of before taking a cruise-ship job is the living situation and how your status on the ship affects it. Cruise ships have different levels of employees. The lowest levels have to share their cabins with three other occupants in a room not much larger than your bathroom at home. They also have the tightest restrictions on where they can go around the ship. They aren't allowed to eat at certain restaurants and can only be on certain decks at certain hours. Essentially, they don't want you mingling with the guests on the ship.

The higher-level employees have more freedom. They either get two-person cabins or single cabins. They are free to go to the guest restaurants and roam about the ship. This is obviously where you want to be. However, there is a common practice between cruise lines that I do not agree with at all. Often times singers and dancers are not looked at equally. Singers would be given the higher-level access and the dancers would be given lower-level. This is because years ago when they started putting entertainment on ships, it used to be just women in evening gowns and men in tuxes singing and you might have a pas de deux. It's now evolved into large song and dance revues where the dancers are prominently showcased, yet they are still treated and paid like extras. Quite honestly, they work much harder than the singers and get the short end of the stick if they don't know this information.

I am by no means trying to dissuade you from taking a cruise-ship job. They are a fantastic way to save a lot of money and really hone your skills as a performer. However, you must negotiate your contract so that you aren't doing any more than your performance job, have better living quarters, and higher-level employee access. If you can negotiate these perks (which I will explain later in this book), your experience will be much greater and you'll be able to fully enjoy your performance contract.

CHILDREN'S THEATRE

"The Little Engine That Could...But Probably Doesn't Want To."

At some point during your career you will probably run into the opportunity to do children's theatre. You'll get to travel the country (and sometimes internationally) to teach workshops and perform shows for schools and arts centers. You'll get to interact with kids and share the joy of doing theatre with them. It can be a very rewarding experience, especially if you have a soft spot for kids.

However, the consistency of children's theatre companies is somewhat across the board. You have some companies that are on the higher quality of production and benefits; such as, housing, traveling, and daily needs. Some are as simple as riding around in a truck along with another person with some flats in the back and staying at host houses. There are more of the latter than the former. So, make sure when you are offered one of these contracts, you know exactly what you are signing up for.

From the majority of stories I've been told, I can conclude most children's theatres (save big budget companies where they only perform in a traditional theatres for family audiences) operate on similar set-ups. You travel to wherever you are scheduled and stay for a couple of days or a week at the time. Sometimes, depending on the company, you may only stay one day and drive to your next destination that night. During this time, you work around 6-8 hour days teaching workshops, doing auditions, and practicing for the show that you perform with the kids at the end of the week. You sometimes stay in hotels and sometimes you stay with a host family. The pay is on the lower end compared to other venues, such as, regional theatres or theme parks and you have very little benefits. Your travel and housing are covered but with very little allowance for variation. Once again, this can vary depending on what company you are working with. Some companies have better setups than others.

I have a colleague who was doing a children's theatre contract with one other tour partner, and they drove a truck across country for about five months. During the winter months they were driving through the northeast and got caught in a snowstorm and needed to postpone their travel. They thought about being the "Little Engine That Could"[9], and fight through the snowstorm and ultimately put themselves at risk, but they really didn't want to. Unfortunately, they were only reimbursed for part of their expenses because of the tight travel allowance. So they ended up having to split the hotel/travel expenses with their own money. Fortunately, this was the only incident they ran into. If they had run into other inclement weather or travel problems at another time, they would have had to do the same thing. Which could be a tremendous burden due to the low pay scale as it is.

So the biggest thing to consider before taking a children's theatre contract is to clarify who pays for incidents such as that and your housing. Those are the two biggest expenses for any performer/technician and you want to make sure you aren't stuck footing the bill for both. If you're offered a tour like the one I just gave an example of, you should also ask about time off for holidays, who is in charge of driving, what your technical duties are, if they have worker's comp, and how long they expect you to travel on any given day. It's very easy to be taken advantage of if you don't cover your bases before hand. So make sure you read the fine print and ask questions. It will save you a lot of headaches in the long run.

REGIONAL THEATRE

"The Sun Will Come Out Tomorrow!"[10]

Regional theatres are the most prevalent in terms of theatre work and every theatre is different in terms of structure. First, you have union houses that work off of LORT (League of Regional Theatre's) contracts. Then you have some union houses that work with both union Guest Artists contracts and non-union actors, and you have non-union regional theatres. A good portion of the theatres you see at unified auditions are non-union. And the quality of work really runs the gambit.

Non-Union regional theatres are a great place to get started because you can do a variety of different roles in a short amount of time, especially if you are doing summer stock. There are some non-union theatres that do really quality work and some theatres that are on the lower end of production quality. Make sure, as a professional, you are working in a quality theatre you aren't ashamed to put on your résumé. Of course, we all have those we don't want to talk about, but we at least try to keep them at a minimum.

There are a good deal of non-union regional theatres, especially repertory theatres, that require their performers and technicians to do things far and beyond just their usual jobs. Many repertory theatres only hire a handful of technical staff and have the actors pick up the slack. So often times, actors will go from rehearsing for 5-6 hours during the morning and afternoon, then do a few hours in the scene shops, then take an hour dinner break and perform that night. So if you're doing a season of five shows in rep, you could be in rehearsal for 6-7 weeks straight.

The wording in the contracts can be somewhat vague and never specify the days you have off. This way you might have the day off from rehearsal, but will still be required to work on the scene shop. Or for technicians, you may be asked to do duties that you were never assigned to, such as the sound technician being asked to take time away from his job to help pick up slack on the scene painting.

After a few weeks of this, you'll be thinking to yourself, "Hopefully, the sun will come out tomorrow!" and you'll be completely burned out by the process once everything it completed. So when you get offers from these companies, make sure you specify that you have certain days off and what you will be asked to do beyond your required duties.

Make sure you're never asked to do additional work that isn't specified in your contract without the proper compensation. Unfortunately, many companies will take advantage of their actors and technicians by asking them to help pick up slack elsewhere. This is totally unfair and unprofessional. If you hired someone to paint one room in your house and then asked them to also paint your hallway, don't expect them to do it out of charity. They are going to charge you for it. So why should your job be any different? It's not, and make sure no one takes advantage of you.

When it comes to union houses and those companies with guest contracts, you start to see some changes. For one, many union houses will allow non-union actors in the Equity Membership Program to receive points to gain admittance into the union. The job requirements are also very defined, so you don't see a lot of crossover between jobs. Very rarely will you see the actors painting the scenery.

Some regional theatres are limited in the amount of union contracts they can offer; depending on the setup they have with the union. There are some higher-end regional theatres that hire union members exclusively. These contracts are just as competitive as any show in New York because they hire from the same pool of people.

With the exception of some of the higher-end regional theatres, the pay for union houses around the country (especially those offering just guest artist contracts) can be significantly less than other venues, such as cruise ships. I'm not saying they aren't livable wages; you can live on those paychecks with relative ease. However, they might not be enough to cover everything you need especially if you have large debts you need to pay off. There really is no rule here that's always true; you have to evaluate each contract on a case-to-case basis.

So the take away from this section is make sure you know exactly what is expected from your contract and clarify any gray areas that could trap you into doing more work without the proper compensation.

TOURS

"On The Road Again..."

Tours come in all sorts of varieties. You have non-union and union tours. You have Bus and Truck tours. You have even smaller tours that I call DIY tours, "Do It Yourself," where you literally do everything from setup and performing (much like many children's theatres). Each has their advantages and disadvantages. For this particular section, I'm going to focus on Bus and Truck tours. The reason being they are a bit more involved and many DIY tours are much like children theatre tours that I discussed earlier. Bus and Truck tours can be both union and non-union and many times have the same benefits. I'll get into union verses non-union later in the book.

Bus and Truck tours can be nice depending on what company you are going out with. They have designated days off, designated travel days, and they work much like any regional union house you may find around the country. They are free during the day unless they have brush-up rehearsal, which in many companies doesn't exceed eight hours a week. They perform mainly at night with only a couple of matinees throughout the week. There are very few overlaps when it comes to job titles (for example, the master electrician won't be painting the scenery) and the schedule is a lot more conducive to great work because you aren't working 12-hour days several days in a row.

These types of tours often try to schedule tour stops within relative distance from one another. This way, on your travel days, you aren't expected to travel for 13 hours from Charlotte, North Carolina to Dallas, Texas to get a show up the next day. I'm not saying that never happens, but it's definitely the exception and not the rule.

A colleague and good friend of mine was once a lead in the national tour of a very popular Disney musical (I'm withholding the name and show for contractual reasons) and the deal she made with this company, using the same techniques I lay out in this book was comparable to equity tours and even some Broadway shows.

Her schedule was six days a week, which some of those days were set aside for travel so they could have a true day off. Her salary was in the $1000-$1500 a week range, plus an added $550 a week per diem. She was contracted for nine performances a week, and if it went over nine by some chance, she would get paid 1/8 of their salary per added show.

In addition to the salary, she got a $50 a week sign-off bonus, so if she toured for one year (52 weeks) she would receive an additional $2,600 at the end of their contract.

As for benefits, the company received $50 a week health fund (to pay for their own private insurance), plus worker's comp, if needed. All transportation and housing is provided and she was assigned an understudy if she were sick with no cut in pay within the allotted time limit.

The company was required to do weigh-ins to make sure they remain the same size as when they were hired, and they were asked to be available for publicity when needed. Not a bad deal for a non-union touring gig. It's all about knowing your worth and knowing how to do business. She used the techniques in this book and got a very cool deal out of it. Not to mention, a leading role in a national tour. I call that a win.

GRAD SCHOOL

"The more you learn..."

Warren Buffett once said, "the more you learn, the more you earn."[11] Now this is true, the only problem is he didn't say *what* you had to learn. I'll let you in on a little secret; you won't learn it from getting a higher degree. Now, I'm not saying grad school is a bad thing but I am saying make sure your judgment is not clouded when you decide to make that choice.

You go to grad school for two reasons. The first, to broaden your horizons to learn something you do not already know (such as a different subject from your undergrad). Second, to deepen your knowledge of your undergraduate degree in order to teach. Note that I did *not* say get a graduate degree in order to get better jobs. Because in this business, it truly does not matter. I'm not saying training is a bad thing (I personally believe it's a constant necessity), but putting yourself in debt to get a higher degree in hopes you might find a better paying/ performing/ directing/designing job is a very short-sighted choice. In reality, you're making the mountain harder and higher to climb for yourself. Not only will you still be competing with the same groups of people, you'll also have a huge debt to pay back. And that's assuming you've already paid your undergraduate student loans off, as well.

So, before you decide to make that choice and get a graduate degree, really think about what you want out of life. Do you want to teach at a college level? By all means, get the degree because you won't be able to teach otherwise. Do you want to perform and work professionally for a living and have no desire to teach college? Then don't put yourself up against a wall with massive student debt and waste years in school instead of going out in the world and making some headway. You can get high-quality training for a fraction of the cost and time elsewhere, such as casting workshops and private lessons.

I have two good examples of my reasoning here. The first deals with a good colleague of mine. He's perhaps one of the greatest jazz singers and showman that I know. He truly knows how to entertain an entire crowd with just himself and a microphone. He moved out to LA and was becoming very discouraged because of the lack of opportunities afforded to him.

There were all sorts of excuses he heard like "you don't have the experience" or "we're looking for someone with more credits." Pretty much all the lines you hear from people hiring. He approached me and told me he was planning on going to grad school for musical theatre (which he also has his undergrad in). I asked him if he wanted to teach and he replied "no." I asked him why he wanted to get his Masters degree and he said, "to at least get noticed by casting directors and producers."

I told him that's very flawed logic because look back at other people he's worked with that had their masters. Did they have a better job? No, they had the same job he did as a performer. Did they get paid better? No, they got paid the same amount as him. Then I told him to think about what he would really learn. At the time of writing this book, there was only one masters degree program in musical theatre performance. His undergraduate professor went there to get his masters.

Essentially, everything he was taught in his undergraduate is the same information his professor received in his graduate. So by that logic, he would literally be paying for nothing but the piece of paper, because he already had the knowledge. Doesn't make a lot of sense, does it? So, I told him maybe the answers he was looking for aren't in school but in self-development.

Well, he took that and ran with it. Using the same information in this book, about marketing, networking, and building your base; he not only beat the same barriers he perceived were holding him back, he is also thriving now. He works only as a performer touring his own show, has paid off all his debt, and is happier than ever while continually building his network and financial base.

Like I said, graduate school is not a bad thing. Just make sure you are doing it for the right reasons.

WORKSHOPS AND MASTERCLASSES

"So this new casting director is doing this workshop...and we should totally go!"

If I had a dollar every time I heard this, I could buy a new Porsche. It happens everywhere, especially in LA and New York. Actors will see this new casting director doing a workshop to help them "really define their type" and "make a better impression" at their audition. It all sounds good and you think you're going to make some good connections, but you realize once you go and spend a couple of hundred dollars, you didn't actually learn anything worthwhile at all. Plus, the class had 35 people in it, and you didn't get any individual attention.

You have to be very careful which workshops and master classes you decide to take and make sure you are not paying for them with the sole purpose of making connections. Nine times out of ten, you will be very disappointed if that's the only reason you go. The types of classes you should be paying for are the ones that teach you skills that you can use to better your craft and make you a better performer/director/designer or that teach you things that help you get better jobs and make you more marketable.

When I hear someone say, "This new casting director is doing a workshop," I hear two things. One, they are doing these classes to make a living and not as some sort of public service. Two, especially if they are a newer director or designer, they probably don't know anything more than you, but they have figured out a way to get your money and finance their lifestyle.

So, unless you are paying for individual time with someone reputable, be weary of throwing money at them.

I once had a friend that moved to New York right out of college with a $30,000 gift from her grandparents to help launch her career. She was very talented and had a great personality. She blew all of that money in two years and is no further than where she started when she moved there. She took all of these classes for the sole purpose of making connections, not furthering herself or her craft, and it got her nowhere. If someone wants you to pay for networking, they are just scamming money off of you. She fell into this trap, as do many others, and is still working as a waitress struggling to make ends meet. If she had spent that money on something that was actionable on her end, such as, learning to market herself or learning to negotiate contracts, I guarantee her situation would be radically different from where she is now.

Understand one thing, I'm not trying to discourage you from taking classes to help hone your craft. As I've stated earlier in the book, I think it's a necessity to have training and to keep training. It will keep you on top of your game and you always want to be the best you can be. What I am saying is be careful who you let take your money. If you want to take vocal lessons for the sake of becoming a better singer, do it. If you want to take classes on new sound technology, go for it. Just make sure you are taking these classes because you actually want to learn what is being taught. If you are arbitrarily taking classes for the sole purpose of trying to make connections, you will end up throwing your money into an endless black hole.

Talk is cheap and the bigger the city, the cheaper the talk. I also knew a guy in LA that would go to a lot of mixers and parties in Hollywood that you had to pay to attend. He was literally paying to go mingle and talk with people. Sounds a little absurd, doesn't it?

He told me he would have great conversations with people but rarely made any lasting connections that had any sort of follow-through. They would say things like, "Oh yea, just email me and send me your stuff. I know so-and-so from working on this project last spring and I'll forward your résumé to him!" It was all sugar-coated BS. Most of the time, they won't forward your email or even open it themselves. All you're left with is their business card and contact info, and when you do try to contact them, it will seem like your talk never happened.

Why am I going on about this? Because of one simple truth. The truth of the matter is that you, and only you, can get the job done. Do not rely on anyone else's promise that they will connect you. That responsibility rests squarely on your shoulders. You need to find out who you need to talk to and get things happening. This is taking an actionable step on your part. Doing this puts you in control. Don't leave your career up to someone else. Don't wait for their people to call your people because that call will never come. Take the initiative and figure out what you want and who you need to contact to get it. You might surprise yourself when you take this on, because you'll see how much further you can go when you are the one in control.

KNOW YOUR MARKET

Now that we've talked about all the different types of venues and job opportunities, it's time to get into the real nuts and bolts: figuring out your market and getting the best job and pay that you possibly can. If you follow the tricks and guidelines I'm about to lay out for you, I guarantee you're going to see a change in your career and your life.

My goal for this section of the book is to give you a comprehensive blueprint on how to find the best jobs for you, how to market yourself for those jobs using the tools readily available to you, and what to do once the money starts rolling in. I'm going to give you practical *actionable* steps to take control of your career, your finances, and your overall fulfillment in this business.

My hope is that after you read this, you will not think of your life and career like the rest of the masses waiting for a lucky break, but as an artist with an entrepreneurial spirit to create their own luck and opportunities. I want you to feel empowered to take the reins of your career and tell it where to go. You have the power to make it happen. I'm going to give you the tools and insights to guide you along the way.

Now think about this. There is a market for literally everything. If you're a singer and you just want to park and bark, there's a venue for that. If you want to be a Shakespearean actor, there's a venue for that. If you're a paraplegic juggler, that also has a knack for training cats, there's a venue for that too. You just have to know which one you belong in.

If you're a pop-belter, don't go auditioning for legit shows. You should focus your energy on the markets that will exhibit your strengths; such as, rock shows, or cruise ships and theme parks. If you're a character actor, feed into that. If you stick to what you're good at, the casting directors will not only notice but appreciate you more. There is nothing worse than someone whose been told, "you just need to go in for everything because you never know," coming into an audition trying to be someone they're not. I'm looking at the opera singers coming into audition for *Rock of Ages* (yes, that actually happens).

The problem is everyone in the world is trying to be good at everything. While it's good to be well-rounded, you need to know your strengths and play to those because that's what is going to get you noticed, which translates into work.

Peter Drucker, the famous management consultant who is referred to as "the father of modern management," in his book *Managing Oneself,* describes this phenomenon.

In his book, he states that all skills can be ranked from 1-100, 100 being the best. He goes on to say that in order to be truly successful (and fulfilled) you must find the skills in yourself that lie between 95-100. The problem is either a) most people don't know what they are good at (are you a better singer than actor?) or b) they fight against what they were predisposed to do.[12]

Take Michael Jordan for instance. After his award-winning streak in basketball, he decided to become a baseball player. You would think a highly-trained athlete like Michael Jordan would do well switching sports, wouldn't you? It was quite the opposite. He only lasted a year. Why? Because he was not predisposed to be a baseball player, he was built to be a basketball player. His height alone would be a complete disadvantage to him playing baseball because his strike zone would be far too big.

So when he started training as a basketball player, he was starting at a 65 on the scale. Because of his height and athleticism, on top of his natural ability to pick up basketball, his training put him at 100 on the scale.

Now if he had started with baseball, which he was not predisposed to do, he would have started at a 10 on the scale. With constant training, he could have gotten to a 65 on the success scale, but not much higher because he wasn't built for baseball. Basketball was his destiny and now he's in the hall of fame for it. He built upon his natural strengths and not his weaknesses.[22]

Unfortunately, most people start with the skills they rank the lowest on, instead of skills that start higher on the success scale. So how do you figure out which ones to focus on? You can use the Eulerian Destiny Theory.

The term Eulerian comes from the mathematical term Eulerian Graph. Think about it like the graph where the circles overlap showing you comparisons and contrasts. In order to figure out what you are truly gifted in, you have to ask four main questions, each representing a circle on the graph. Where they all overlap is what you need to concentrate on.

The first circle will be about the environment that you grew up in. What did your parents do? What type of classmates did you have? This will give you insight on who you are as a person. If your parents where in management, you probably have a knack for that as well, and maybe have talents in directing or writing. Look at your friend circle. Were you and your friends the class clowns? Maybe you have a knack for comedy or acting. Were your friends the bookworm type? Maybe you have knack for writing shows.

The second circle is something called the stranger bias. This is feedback from complete strangers. When you perform, what do they comment on the most? Your voice? Your acting? This is a great indicator of what your talents are. If you're a writer, do people commend you on your comedy or how well you construct a really strong emotional scene? The stranger bias is a great indicator of your strengths because unlike friends, they have no incentive to lie to you.

The third circle is what you have been doing the past 5-10 years. Even if you aren't in your ideal career, you still have experience from your past endeavors. What stands out to you the most?

The fourth circle is what you can talk about effortlessly for hours. What are you passionate about? What makes you excited in the morning?

Once you take a look at all four of these areas, see where they all intersect. It will take some time and serious brainpower, but

I promise it will help define your true purpose, whether it be in performing, directing, writing, or designing.

Just remember, don't be like the masses and wander aimlessly trying to figure out your purpose. Use the Eulerian Destiny Theory to point you in the right direction. Don't forget, specificity is key.

Once you have figured out what skills you're best at, the ones that can take you to 100 on the success scale, you need to know how to sell them. And that's what we're going to do now.

WEBPAGE AND OTHER PROMOTIONS

The single best and most underrated highway to work is through your webpage. You'll be surprised at how many people take this platform for granted or don't even use it at all. We are living in an age where everything is connected to the internet. I know you hear that often, almost to the point you don't really understand the value of that statement, but it's your single best tool (other than yourself) to promote your art.

Here are a couple of guidelines when it comes to creating your own webpage:

- Do **NOT** be cheap when it comes to creating it. I will say this again because it is so important. Do not be cheap. If you create a website where the address is tylersmith. wix.net, it automatically tells me you spent no money to create it, therefore you do not value yourself as a business. Instead, go to GoDaddy and buy yourself a domain name and website hosting. I recommend GoDaddy because they are often the cheapest hosting platform on top of having excellent customer service. They can walk you through every step to get your website up and running. When you spend money on a professional website, it is creating *value* in yourself and your business and potential producers will in turn value you more.

- Hire a professional designer to make your webpage look good. They aren't horribly expensive and if you can find a designer that is just starting out, even better. A new designer will not only work harder for you but also will want to create a good product, because they will have something to prove. That's an excellent business partnership. The reason you want your product to look good is simple. People will judge a book by its cover. Think about it this way. If you are at Walmart looking for a hairdryer and you see two on the shelf, both the same price, but one is in pretty packaging and one is in a burlap sack, which one are you going to choose? The pretty packaging, of course. It doesn't even matter if the one in the burlap sack works better, because the one that was packaged and promoted properly created value for itself. Moral of the story: don't put yourself in a burlap sack. And this rule goes for <u>everything</u> your name is on.

- Just like everything else in this book, specificity is key. Make sure it's easy to get to and navigate. Keep it clean and concise. No one wants to see extra photos of you tailgating or see your twitter feed about what you did this weekend. Keep all the content about you professional and about your art.

- There are five main pages to have on your website: Bio,

Résumé, Media, Photos, and Booking Information. Make sure these are up-to-date and relevant to your product. Perhaps, even schedule a day every week to check in on your webpage and make sure all the links work, and if anything needs to be updated or cleaned. Stay on top of the game. If you're proactive with this, you will be way ahead of everyone else that became complacent.

- Picasso once said, "Good artists copy, great artists steal." When it comes to advertisements, steal from the best. Look at your Fortune 500 company websites. Look at how Walmart designs its websites, or McDonalds, or Amazon. These companies hire advertisement agencies and psychologists and sociologists to create their websites and advertisements. They have it down to a science (literally!) to get you to buy their products. So, why not use their method of doing things? Look at their websites and take what you think works. It might be the layout or the font or how every page links to one another. Look at a bunch of websites and take pieces and parts from each one you like and show them to your designer to emulate those. The key is to make it as sleek and professional as possible. You don't have to pay a fortune for it, but it should be able to hold its own against the web pages that are household names.

- Also, create a logo of your name. Nothing fancy or extravagant. Just something understated and simple. This way you can put it on everything you use for promotions, from Facebook to business cards.

I said above that your webpage should have five main tabs: Bio, Resume, Media, Photos, and Booking Information. Let's break these down even more, so you have a clearer idea of what should be on each page.

Bio: The most important thing to keep in mind when writing your bio is to keep it short and exciting. I will quote Barney Stinson from, *How I Met Your Mother*, when he made the "Get Psyched CD Mix," "It should be all rise! It should start high and get higher!"[13] Same rule applies to writing a bio, you want to leave them wanting more.

First, you should write it in third person as if someone is writing an article about you. Keep it professional-only talk about your professional gigs. Don't talk about what shows you did in college or high school or about your pet cat. Also, mention special projects you might be working on, like writing a play or composing music, or any other creative outlets. It makes you seem much more intriguing because you are making things happen for yourself.

Once again, keep it professional. The total length on your bio shouldn't be more than three concise paragraphs.

Résumé: Your résumé should be sleek, clean, and to the point. Almost like a flyer you hand out on your professional work. Just give highlights – you don't need everything you have done on it. Odds are after you read this book; you won't have room to put it all anyway.

Forget the dates – just line up your credits with the latest gig at the top. Odds are, as a director, I'm only going to read the first two entries anyway, because I'm more interested in what you're about to do in the audition, rather than read the résumé you just handed me.

There is also no need to name-drop, because if the casting director or whoever is hiring knows a company you've worked for, they will know the people. Odds are they will probably ask you about them.

Now, this next part might sound controversial, but what's good advice without a little drama? This tip really only applies to those just starting out in the business but color your résumé, if need be, to make it sound as professional as possible. I'm not telling you to lie, but I am telling you to sound legitimate. So, if you're just starting out and you've only done community theatre, instead of saying "Farmville Community Theatre" say the actual name of the theatre itself like the "Paramount Theatre." If the person hiring doesn't know it, they probably won't ask. If they do ask, you tell them it was a theatre back in Kansas (or wherever you're from). Once again, not a lie, it's just framed differently.

Make sure you check all your grammar and spelling, as well as, have all the title of shows italicized. Make sure you take the time to proofread and have a friend proofread, because if you have mistakes on your résumé, it makes you look sloppy and unintelligent.

Make sure your contact info is on every piece of promotional material you have and that it is up-to-date. If you are just out of school, do not use a school email address; nine times out of ten the school will cancel them after graduation. Plus, using a school address, a Gmail account, or any other email, that is not your domain name, looks unprofessional. When you buy website hosting, many times it will come with an email address (i.e. Rachel@rachelsmith.com). Not only is it easy to use, but it also makes you look way more professional. There is absolutely no excuse for you not to have a professional email address in this day and time. If you want to be disconnected from technology, you are in the wrong career.

Media: You need to have four reels, depending on what you do. If you're an actor/singer have a musical theatre reel, a pop/rock reel, TV/Film reel, and a dance reel. Do not put all these together into one reel; no one, except your great aunt, is going to watch it all.

Many times when directors ask for reels, they are looking for one very specific thing. So don't inundate them with extra material. If they want to see you belt your face off, don't make them sit through two minutes of your dance reel before you start singing. This is why it's smart to separate them out.

Keep the individual reels at about two and a half minutes, absolutely no more than 3. You really have to assume you're sending your reel to someone with a very short attention span. Keep it tight and keep it exciting. Just like your bio, it should be "all rise." You need to maximize your strengths while limiting your weaknesses. When the video is done, they should have the feeling of wanting even more.

Just give them the highlights of the song. No one wants to hear the part of *Defying Gravity* before the line, "It's meeee!"[14] They want the money notes. The same rule applies to your acting reel. Give them about 7-8 seconds before the climax of the scene. For a dance reel, start with your best tricks to get them excited and then show them your technique. The secret here is to start big and get bigger and to make it seem like it just can't get any better. Most casting directors won't even watch a whole minute of your reel, so grab their attention and go higher.

Just like the website, do not skimp on quality. When you have videos made, use multi-angle videos with professional sound and lighting. Everyone in the business judges a book by its cover and the nicest looking packaging gets the most attention. Once again, you don't have to spend a fortune. Find someone just starting out that has a good work ethic. What you're filming is relativity easy and doesn't require a lot of production…just well-executed simplicity. So finding someone decent shouldn't be hard, just ask around.

Also, don't forget to add your contact info and logo. You want your video to look the same as everything else you put out. So make sure your fonts, logo, spellings, everything is consistent across all mediums.

Photos: You need to have 2 sections of photos, one of headshots and the other of production stills. And of course, all of these photos should be professionally done. You get what you pay for, so just like your website and video reels, don't skimp out on quality.

You should not have any personal photos on your website, such as, photos taken with your iPad or cell phone. For sure, you should not put any selfies on your website.

Your photos should not only look like you, but they should capture your personality. Unfortunately, we are not a good judge of ourselves, so poll your friends and see which ones really show who you are. It's going to be someone else that judges your headshot anyway, so you might as well let other people tell you which one works the best.

You should also take new photos at least once every two years and never keep your old headshots up. They mislead people and that's the last thing you want to do. We change little by little every year and you want to stay consistent with your photos.

Casting directors look at thousands of thumbnails everyday, so be sure to use solid colors and stay away from busy backgrounds or anything that distracts the eye away from you. Your eyes, in close up headshots, should be engaged and seem to pop.

Stay away from too much airbrushing and touch up. You can digitally remove zits in a headshot (because that's what they use make-up for) but if you have something such as scars or a slight deformity; just leave it. That scar might actually help you get a job. Plus, it keeps your headshots natural and a true representation of you.

The most important thing about a headshot is that it shows who you really are and captures your essence. If you find yourself looking at the camera and you're not sure how to smile, I'll give you one of the most helpful pieces of advice I've ever received. Look directly at the camera and smile as if you have a secret you're keeping from the person taking the photos. It engages your eyes, gives you a great smile, and gives you a great point of view.

Booking Information: Just like every other part, keep it clean, simple, and straightforward. Make sure you have a permanent address that will never change, even if it's a PO box, so that you can always be contacted. Have your phone number and email address up to date, but nothing else. So, no Facebook or Twitter handles. You can put those widgets on the front page of your website.

If you have an agent or manager, be sure to also put their appropriate contact information first.

Most importantly, make sure your voicemail is activated and always has space. You'll be surprised how many times I will call someone with a job offer and couldn't leave a voicemail. It's not very professional, and it looks bad on your part.

SOCIAL MEDIA

All the social media platforms play by the same rules as traditional marketing; meaning that, your brand must be the same throughout all your different platforms. Consistency is key here, so make sure you have all the same photos, logos, fonts, etc., consistent between all the different social media platforms.

Once again, you need to take from the best. Look at the social media platforms of big companies or famous products. Look at all of them objectively and see what they have in common. I'll give you a couple of freebies right now.

Take McDonalds Instagram for example. You'll notice that they don't just post photos of their food. Actually, they rarely post photos of any food at all. I would say roughly 10% of their content is actually related to what they are selling, the rest are photos of happy couples splitting some fries or two guys on skateboards drinking some coffee. Why do you think that is? Because it's not the product itself that makes it sell, it's the life (presumably) you will get if you buy their product. They are appealing to your emotional side, which for a majority of people is the driving force behind their decisions.

Think about the commercials you see on TV for Sandals resorts. It's showing you images of happy couples playing on the beach and a quite romantic dinner by themselves under a canopy with no one around. Do you think the real experience is that heightened? Probably not, but you *want* it to be, so you buy into it.

So how does McDonalds and Sandals resort relate to you? You use their same tactics when using your social media platforms.

Once you post on any platform (Twitter, Instagram, Facebook, etc.), don't just post about you and take endless selfies of yourself in rehearsal. Instead, use the 10%/90% rule, 10% you (what you're selling) and 90% the environment that comes with hiring you (the couple sharing fries on a park bench). So, when you get a big gig, of course, you can post that but don't post every gig you get. Instead, show photos of theatres you're working in or of great designs of your friends and link them into everything you do, as well. Not only are you promoting yourself but also your friends, who in turn get more people to promote you. It's a win/win, plus it makes you look like an awesome person.

Stay away from controversial matters and keep everything positive. Don't post any of your personal life (unless it directly relates to your business) and be disciplined to post often with great quality and consistency.

You want to be able to link yourself to anyone in your field or a relatable field. So, if you're a lighting designer and you see some great work a friend of yours has done, a good post on any platform would read, "Hey guys! Look at this great design by @

lightingguy! He's doing @thismusical at @thistheatre. Make sure you tell him how much you like the design, I know he'd love to hear from you!"

I know this post might seem a little silly but let's read into it a bit more. If you're a lighting designer and you show support for another fellow designer, that's just goodwill points and everyone loves to be supported and feel good. You've also linked him to your social media platforms. You've also mentioned the musical and theatre in your post, linking fans of both to not only your friend but also to you. Then the phrase, "Make sure you tell him how much you like the design," opens your post to positive comments, which then helps him and you gain notoriety by bringing more people in and getting them engaged.

One of the best pieces of advice about this subject is by Dale Carnegie, author of *How to Win Friends and Influence People*. He was on the forefront of self-improvement and how it relates to salesmanship and interpersonal skills. He said, "you can make more friends in two months by becoming more interested in other people than you can in two years by trying to get people interested in you."[15] Think about that. Most people in this business are very egocentric and that's not a good way to sell yourself, but if you become innately interested in people (like the example of the previous post) you will make way more friends; and that translates into work because people want to work with their friends. It may sound crazy, but try it, and I guarantee you will see results.

Now that we've covered the basics, lets get into some do's and don'ts of some of the bigger social media platforms.

Facebook: To think that Facebook started out as a college "hot or not" website and has now turned into a tool in which anyone and everyone can communicate with each other is a testament to how powerful social media can be. It went from a college based website to one of the most popular websites on the planet in a very short time.[23]

So, if you don't have a Facebook page promoting yourself, it will just seem strange. Make sure your personal and your professional pages are completely separate. You want your professional page to be a platform that other like-minded professionals in your business can communicate with each other. Not a page that people can comment on about what your dinner looks like that night.

I would suggest syncing your Facebook, Instagram, and Twitter together. This way all your posts are consistent across the board. Be sure to post at least twice a day, using the rules stated earlier, in order to keep your audience up to date.

Facebook is going to be your most prominent social media platform, solely because it's the most prevalent and all other platforms can link back to it. Make sure to keep it active and full of content related to your field, not just you.

Twitter: Twitter is a great networking tool if you use it properly. Using the same principles I spoke of earlier about bringing your friends and colleagues into the mix by cross-promoting is a great advantage most people are not using. Make sure when you tweet, you link people and other prevalent businesses/companies/etc. to yourself. If you sync all your social media platforms, you will increase your visibility up to four times more than you would using a single platform.

Unfortunately, many places (especially those in the music

business looking to sign on artists) look to see how active you are on social media. More importantly, they want to know how many followers you have and how engaged they are with you and your product.

I've known people that have come very close to signing deals with some excellent record labels because their product was so good and they were persistent in getting to know the right people, only to be turned away because their "base" was not big enough. What a pity to get in the door only to be turned away, because you weren't active enough on social media. It just goes to show how strong the platform is.

It's nothing to get stressed over, because contrary to popular belief, it is easy to get followers. Use the principles I talked about earlier and read books on the subject to further your knowledge. Just remember, 10% content of you, and 90% content that is relative to your audience. Ask them questions and get them involved. Post inspiring photos and videos. Re-Tweet like-minded people. When someone follows you, follow him or her back; especially if they are someone you are interested in meeting or working with. You have complete control over it.

Now this brings up the question, "do I buy followers or not?" There are benefits and downsides to this. There are companies out there that offer fake followers for as little as $10 for 1,000 followers. However, social media sites are really cracking down on getting rid of spam accounts, so your numbers could be in the thousands one day and back down to 200 the next. Some companies offer warranties but I wouldn't trust it.

My initial reaction is no, you never need to buy followers. You can build it up on your own in a relatively short time. However, in the *very* rare circumstance that Capitol Records calls you out of the blue and asks for a meeting, and you need some followers in a hurry, then I would definitely consider it. I've never come across such an instance, but never say never. Even if you have tens of thousands of followers or just a couple of hundred, still be active and build up your base.

Instagram: Instagram is essentially the picture version of twitter so the same rules apply, however, there are a few key differences we'll talk about.

Instagram does not allow you to post web links in your postings, however, you are allowed to link in your bio. So make sure you put your website address in your bio and drive traffic to your website.

Make sure you put all your social media handles in your bio, as well as, link Instagram to all your social media platforms. This way all your posts are connected, and if someone just happens upon your Instagram, they can easily find your other platforms, as well.

Be sure the picture quality is consistent. You want your self-image to be one that is clean and presented well, so don't post a lot of haphazard selfies and pictures of you driving around in your car. Instead, post professional quality photos of the venues where you might be working, the marquee with your show's title on it, or other prominent people in the industry. Once again, make sure you tag them all and cross-promote.

YouTube: The golden rule of YouTube is make sure you only have professionally shot and edited videos and make them easy to find. You will have to create a YouTube channel and you want nothing but the best videos showing the best of what you have to offer.

Consistent with the branding we discussed earlier, every video should have your name/logo and website information on it. Remember to think of a McDonald's commercial. They all look the same and you want your videos to have the same consistency and structure. It makes you look organized and professional, and even better, it makes you look established. The more established you seem, the more your value goes up.

Your channel also has an "About" section, so be sure to post your website and all your social media platforms there.

Make sure all your videos are public, especially your performance reels. If you need to record an audition and send it via YouTube, make sure to select "Unlisted" when you upload. This way you can send your link, but only those that have the link can watch it. This keeps your channel from looking cluttered and ensuring only the videos you want the public to watch are displayed.

All Other Professional Media Sites (i.e. LinkedIn, 800Casting, LA Casting, etc.): The same rules apply to all these websites, as they do to your website and social media platforms. You want to make sure everything is consistent, continually updated, and they link back to your website and what you're selling.

These websites are really a whole different money making industry. You can spend thousands trying to get every feature from every website, so make sure you choose wisely when purchasing anything. Only get the essentials of what you really need. We won't get into that topic in this book, because it would take a whole other book to explain it all. However, a good rule of thumb is if it looks like you're spending money on something you don't see a lot of return in or your gut says it's a waste of money, it probably is.

When it comes into other types of promotions, such as, postcards or any other physical promotional materials you may need, just keep the rules in mind. Once again, consistency is key.

I'm also a big fan of business cards. It may seem a little old school, but it's a great tool to exchange information when you first meet someone. Plus, it's very classy in the old-school sense.

You can go to Vistaprint online and get great deals on bulk business cards. They even have tools to help you design them. Of course, always go for the custom option and don't choose one that's already pre-designed. That's for boring people with no imagination, which you are not!

When designing your business cards, the front of the card should just have a headshot, logo, and what you do/what you're selling. And make sure to blend the headshot into the rest of the background, so it doesn't look like a license photo just tacked onto a card. On the back, you should have your contact information, as well as, a QR code that sends them to your website. Getting a QR code is easy, just google "QR code generator" and there are a thousand websites that do it for free.

If you want to get really fancy and you find yourself going to a lot of different mixers and meeting new people in your business, it might be good to have business cards that are consistently updated. The best example of this is a good colleague of mine out in LA, who performs all around downtown and in Hollywood. He prints about 100 business cards every month and puts an abbreviated performance schedule of his upcoming gigs on the back. He, of course, has all the info mentioned earlier, but he also lists the dates/times/venues when he is performing. He says this technique has tripled the size of his base, as well as, performance opportunities, because more people are coming to see him perform.

Promotion opportunities are everywhere; you just have to be creative enough to make them work for you!

NETWORKING

Networking: The single most important word to anyone in any field. The saying goes, "It's not what you know, it's who you know." I can give you one better. It's not so much who you know, but who knows YOU.

Think about it. When you were in school, you were always more inclined to work with your friends, rather than someone you didn't know. This stands true every single day. People want to hire other people they know and trust, more so than a random person that walks into the door.

This is why it takes so many auditions with the same casting director before they eventually cast you. *You have to build a relationship with them.* My friend who went on to play the lead in the national tour of a Disney musical had 11 callbacks before she finally got the job. She didn't go in the audition room with the intention of just doing her best and asking for a job. She went in to establish a relationship with the casting director and the people behind the table.

Over the course of time, she became friends with the casting director. Not because she wanted a job, but because he was a genuinely nice man. She herself never actually asked about a job. Remember the quote from earlier by Dale Carnegie; you can make more friends being interested in other people than trying to get them interested in yourself[15]. This is the secret to success in all things. It's a "trick" that will never prove wrong.

Networking really should be called something else. Networking implies "business" like stigmas. Instead, simply think about making friends. And you don't make friends by trying to get people to do things for you. So, with every person you meet; ask yourself what you can give them instead of what they can give you. You'll be surprised how quickly your luck will turn around.

Unfortunately, most people meet someone that could potentially help them get a job or make a professional connection, and they immediately start talking about themselves and seeing what the other person can give them. We know those types of people. They're the people that follow you down the street begging for change. What do you do when you run into people like that? You keep walking and ignore them. It's human nature.

Instead of being the one begging for change, ask yourself what you can give to that person. First, ask them about themselves, people absolutely love to talk about themselves. It's really a logical fallacy because people love to talk about themselves, however they dislike people that do nothing but talk about themselves. So, don't be that person and become an active listener instead.

When relating to people, I have one thing that always stands true. Everyone has a sign around their neck that says, "Make me feel good." It's up to you to figure out how. Everyone has a passion they love to talk about. Be well-read and be able to hold a conversation about all different types of topics, enough so that you can at least ask intelligent questions. This will impress people more than anything. Imagine you're an actor and go into an auto shop to get your oil changed. The mechanic asks what you do and you tell him you're an actor. He then replies, "That's really cool, I've always been amazed by Shakespeare and how he wrote in iambic pentameter. How do you think he did it?" Not only would you be really impressed, you would make sure to go back to him again, because he actively tries to relate to you.

The cool thing about this is that it applies to *everyone* and *every* situation. Another trick to help you relate to people and make new friends is to figure out their dominant traits and play up to that. Everyone's personality has four categories: *action, planning, emotional, and social. Action* people are the "screw it, let's just make it happen" type of people. *Planning* types are more reserved and feel the need to plan every event in their lives, really the antithesis of a truly *action* personality. *Emotional* people tend to tie every aspect of their life to an emotional response, such as, "the train ride from Brooklyn made me really depressed, but then I came into the bar and was much happier." They explain everything through emotion. The *social* types of people are very much "go with the flow." They sort of go wherever the crowd goes and typically get along with everyone. Everyone has bits of pieces of each category in their personality; it's up to you to find the most dominate.

For example, you would not ask a *planning*-type of person to jump in the car and go somewhere without knowing what was happening first. If you're a *planning*-type of person, you certainly don't want to try to tie down a *social*-type, because they won't respond well and will be left disappointed. You certainly don't want to try to have a theoretical conversation with a highly *emotional* person, because they won't understand you.

Your job is to figure out which personality trait is dominant in the other person and then bring that side of you out. This makes the other person more comfortable with you, as well as, makes you more relatable to them. That's the secret to making friends with anyone.

Now remember, there is a fine line between promoting yourself and being a cocky, arrogant, selfish person. You can stay clear of that just by remembering the tricks I just mentioned and remember everyone has the sign, "make me feel good", around their neck. You can never give too much. For instance, it's much classier to buy someone a drink than to give them a simple handshake. It shows you're willing to give and not just take when it's convenient for you. Remember, whatever you give in the world will be paid back to you ten times over. You must give to receive.

You don't give Christmas presents with the expectation of getting something back, so why should it be any different in any other aspect of your life? Giving with the intention of getting something back is very unattractive. Give to people because you want to, not because you need to.

The biggest networking opportunity is that of the people you work with. This cannot be overstated. Your colleagues are your biggest networking assets. You can work the rest of your life, or not at all, depending on how well you treat and work with others. The show business community is small and only gets smaller the more you work. Word travels fast, so be sure you're the person someone would suggest for a project.

When someone contacts me for a referral, I will always suggest reputable individuals that I know. However, there are some individuals that I would never recommend based solely on their lack of work ethic and poor attitude. It really has nothing to do with if you're talented or not. If you've worked before, it means you're talented. I'm much more interested in who you are as a person.

The next point I think is really important and it's very simple: don't be afraid to go talk to people. The difference between successful people and unsuccessful people is a simple three-letter word: **ask**. So, find people you admire and would want to emulate and go talk with them. You'd be surprised how often successful people will take time out of their schedule to help those that are truly interested in learning. If you don't ask, the answer is always no. So there is no harm in asking!

People are social beings and enjoy talking and communicating with other people, unless of course you're anti-social, and if that's the case why are you in this business? Remember to approach everyone as a person and as an equal, even celebrities. They're just normal people with more face time on TV than you.

Connect with all your contacts online and make a list of influential people you know or would want to know. Do some research on what they've done and who they may know. I bet you'll find common connections. Don't be afraid to use them, that's what friends are for!

Another great "ninja trick" for anyone in show business is to align themselves with other mutually beneficial connections.

For instance, actors should align themselves with new directors/ writers/composers. Designers should align themselves with directors and other designers they want to emulate. This way the relationship is mutually beneficial and can carry on to several different projects in the future.

Good examples of this are actresses that align themselves with new composers. The actress helps the new composer with his or her work and oftentimes sings it for them in showcases and other venues to promote their work. They aren't doing it for money, they do it to help a friend out. But in turn, when the composer promotes his or her work, they also are promoting you because you're the one singing the material. And, when you workshop the show and bring on a director and producer, they also become part of your team because you are cross-promoting each other. It's a win/win for everyone. When the show gets sent to Broadway or picked up by a network, guess who is definitely on top of the résumé pile because of the favors you did for your friends?

Again, it's not what you can get, but what you can give that matters. Once you master that, networking will become second nature to you.

AGENTS AND MANAGERS

Agents and managers are a necessary evil, but only *when* they become a necessity. Now, this is not to say agents and managers are evil. Many do really good work as evidenced of those you see on stage and screen. The one thing you don't hear is when it's a good idea to find representation and management, and how to leverage both properly.

A common misconception is that you have to find both, an agent and a manager, in order to find decent work when you're getting started in this business. That couldn't be further from the truth. You can find great work just by doing research on your own, and it costs you less money because you don't have to give a hefty percentage (often 10-15%) to someone else.

Many people believe their first step to finding success in this business is to move to New York or LA and immediately find an agent. This is flawed for a couple of reasons. First, you're going to want a good agent/manager. Why would a good, reputable agency pick up someone without a winning track record? It's too risky. They have their reputation to think about, as well. Second, if you do find an agent right out of the gate, and you have no track record, you're going to find the work you're being sent in for isn't very satisfying, or will not provide you the cash you deserve. So how do you combat this?

The first thing you need to do is build up your résumé and portfolio. Hit the pavement and submit to everything that fits for you. Go to every audition that works for your type. Get jobs that build your résumé and look good on your reel. The idea is to build yourself up to a point those agents and managers are seeking you out. Then they will truly work for you.

A good example of this is my colleague, Eric. He went out to LA with very few credits, but he had one goal in mind and that was to build himself up to the point agents and managers sought him out. So he started out just singing with tracks in some local bars in North Hollywood. Then he became connected with various musicians, and they played around town. After awhile, they were booking bigger and bigger venues just because of their persistence and the track record they had created for themselves.

He even went on to tour with his own show across the country, which further validated him. Once he reached a certain level on his own, various agents and mangers started to come to his shows and afterwards they would ask if he had representation. He found an agency that works for him and is now doing great work. He just finished a series on Fox network, as well as, filmed a movie opposite Tom Hiddleston. This is solely because he built himself up to a higher point, gave himself a winning track record, and now the agency knows his worth and really pushes him for gigs. The agency would not have pushed him if he didn't have a self-made track record, which unfortunately, is a trap many people fall into.

To really understand this, you have to know how agents and managers work. Agents net fish for jobs. They essentially see a posting and send the information of every person they have on their roster that fits the description and hope someone sticks. Managers essentially make sure you, as a business, are covered on all levels. They make sure you're taking the right gigs (and sometimes help you find them), as well as, handling all your promotions, finances, contracts, etc.

Agents get money whenever they get you a job (often 10-15%, as the pay gets higher the percentage sometimes shrinks, that's dependant on the agency). Managers get money from your work no matter what, even if they didn't have a hand in helping you get the gig. Their fee is also around 10-15% of your pay. So make sure before you sign any contract with anyone, you know exactly what is expected of each party and what the percentage of each gig is owed to them. You should *never* have to pay an agent or a manager before you sign with them.

Let's go a little further into these percentages and why it's a good idea to build up your résumé before getting an agent or a manager. Let's say you're fresh to LA or NY. You don't have a lot of savings (if any) and you're hungry for work. You immediately look for an agent to help find you work, but you don't have any proven track record. They send you out for some stuff, not great and not a lot of pay. You also decide to hire a manager to help you promote yourself and get a better grip on this business. So the jobs you book at the beginning maybe pay $500 a week. Take 10% out for your agent, which leaves $450. Now take out 15% for your manager, which leave you $383. Now take out an additional 20% for your state and federal taxes, that leaves you with $306. Now take out your rent, utilities (which in NY and LA is the most expensive in the world), and any debt you may have. You're left with no money to actually live on. So, you pick up another job to make ends meet, but because of the demands of that job you have no time to actually go to auditions, thus, starting the vicious downward spiral. Doesn't sound pleasant, does it?

But, once you start to build up your own résumé and your agency really pushes you for gigs that pay triple and quadruple that, those numbers become livable. The front-end work you do at the beginning will pay dividends on the back half when the agency really works for you.

I hear more often than not, "My agent just isn't sending me in for anything," or, "My agent is sending me in for all the wrong stuff!" Something always struck me as wrong about that. Your agent works for you. You pay them. And in my book, if you pay someone they are your employee, and they do what you want them to do. Do you know of any other industry where the employee tells the boss what to do? Absolutely not! Why should a talent agency be any different?

If you have proven your own track record, you are giving the agency the opportunity to work for you, not the other way around. So don't be flattered and honored when you find people that want to represent you. That's their job and they work for you. Empowering isn't it?

Of course, I'm not saying you should treat anyone with disrespect. An ideal relationship with you and your agent/manager should be one of mutual respect. You want to find someone that will stick with you and work for you in both the good times and the down times. After you build your career, it shouldn't be hard to find an agent/manager that works with you on both a personal and professional level.

You want to find an agent and manager that best suits you and needs your type to fill a gap in their roster of talent. Remember, if you aren't getting paid, they aren't getting paid. You've done your part in building yourself up; it's now their job to push the proven product. And if they aren't working to your satisfaction, you should find someone else. If you've built yourself up, you won't have trouble finding another agency.

There are some telltale signs that you might want to find another agent/manager, or that you have signed on to an agency too soon in your career. If you hear them say, "My phones just aren't ringing," it means I'm not getting off my butt to work any harder for you, or even simpler, they just don't want to deal with you.

If they ask you, "when are you back in town?" that just means they aren't going to submit you for anything until you are there physically and can show up to every audition imaginable, right or wrong for you. If you ever hear, "I know your type better than you do" or "this is big" it means they don't really know you or your product at all, and they are trying to sell you on a gig that might be mediocre at best. To agents, especially speaking to people with no track record, everything is big. And I've known agents to send skinny white girls for parts that call for a larger black lady. No joke, you have to do your research before you agree to do any audition.

You must keep a tight reign on your agent and manager. Remember, they are your employees and they work for you. Make sure you're getting what you pay for. And when you find the right agency at the right time, make sure you still have control of your business and your career. The only person that's going to get you to where you want to go is you. Agencies are merely a tool to help you along the way.

UNIONS

Unions are, and always have been, a highly political subject. Some people are pro-union and some people are strictly against unions. In this section, I'm going to be talking about performance unions, using examples mainly about Actors Equity, which is the union I have the most working knowledge of. I'm a professional music director, and I am neither pro-union nor anti-union. I have no affiliation with any performance union, but I have experience working with union members. So, with that disclosure, I will try to be as objective as possible.

Unions really became prevalent in the United States during the industrial revolution, when working conditions were dismal and wages were well below the poverty line. This was the first time in America where laborers (especially those working in factories with very low safety standards) needed a collective voice to make their jobs livable, and more importantly, safe.

The industrial revolution was when capitalism was at its most unrestrained. So at the time, unions were necessary to keep the balance of unbridled capitalism with the needs of the working middle class. As time has changed and working conditions have evolved, the roll of unions has also changed. The need for unions to leverage their collective power and make better working conditions has been largely replaced by government-sanctioned regulations. The government also sets minimum wage requirements, but salaries are still leveraged to a degree by respective unions, such as, Equity.

What rolls do unions have on your career today? It's gotten a little more complicated.

First, being union under certain conditions has many upsides. For example, if you are living in New York and you receive a production contract, there are several benefits to being in the union. They secure your salary, your work schedule, as well as, secure benefits like health care, sick leave, and a retirement pension[16]. I prefaced this "if you are living in New York" for a reason. The price of living in New York is astronomical in comparison to other parts of the country. When you are under a production contract, it doesn't allow you to pick up a second job to make ends meet either because of time demands or physical demands. Considering the competition in the area, it's great having the security of knowing you can have the one job of performing, while your living expenses and insurance will be taken care of.

When it comes to other parts of the country and you're looking at regional theatres and especially tours, the paradigm starts to shift.

You'll notice that touring productions are now about half equity and half non-equity, more so than it has ever been in the past. Now to give you a complete picture of why this is prevalent, I'll try to explain a little bit of the business behind tours.

When a producer puts up a show, he has to a raise a hypothetical $5 million dollars. It cost him $300,000 to run the show weekly, plus $100,000 to pay back the investors. So to break even, he must make $400,000 within the one-week the show runs at any particular theatre. The presenter (the theatre the tour goes to) will guarantee the producer a hypothetical $400,000 plus 10% of whatever the box office makes. The remainder of the money grossed (after expenses) will be split between the producer and the presenter, hopefully enough to where each party makes a profit. Easy enough, right?[24]

Now you can imagine how difficult it is to make a consistent $400,000 every week to just break even in the current economy. So what does any good business owner do? Lower expenses! This is when non-equity tours come into play.

Because of the financial requirements of hiring all union workers, the running costs go up exponentially. Under certain union contracts (depending on what tier the production falls under) the producer has to not only pay the actors salary, but also contribute to their social security, pensions, 401(k), and the union health insurance. They are also required to hire certain skill level jobs, such as, tutors for juvenile actors[25].

The financial requirements of a non-equity tour are somewhat less of a burden because oftentimes they will hire performers as contractors (they are only taxed at the end of the year instead of every paycheck) and keep their running costs low. The salary is comparable to union contracts (it may be slightly less but not much). The salary would be offset if you don't have agent and manager dues, which is not a requirement to get a national tour, as evidenced by my friend now touring a Disney show. Since you're paid as a contractor, you can do your own taxes, which is ideal in saving money in the long haul, and something I will go into later. With the way healthcare is set up today, you can get a decent private insurance plan for the same amount you could through your employer. In the end, you could make the same amount of money, or more if you're diligent, doing a non-union tour rather than being on a union contract.

As a presenter, if I could get the same quality shows and not have to guarantee such a massive amount up front, I would definitely go for that. It means a better chance of breaking even and making a profit for both the producer and the presenter. Not only that, just as in some union contracts, many non-equity tour producers will split overages with the rest of the company. So once the initial investment is paid off, every actor is guaranteed a percentage of the profits over whatever expenses the producers has, in addition to their guaranteed salary. If the up-front cost is smaller (as it would be for a non-union show), the faster the investment is paid off. Therefore, the producer and everyone else make more money. From a business point of view, that makes sense.

With non-equity productions really coming in as a power player, there is just as much competition for equity roles as there are for non-equity roles. A good example of this would be cruise lines. In the past couple of years they have really started to push name-brand material such as *Hairspray* and *Rock of Ages*, with compensation that is equal, if not more than, what many equity contracts pay. So don't feel like you need to be part of a union to get good pay and benefits. There are tons of non-equity work that offer comparable benefits. You just have to be motivated to find them.

So, should you join a union or not? It really depends on what your goals are and where you priorities lie. There is equal competition on both teams. If you're in film and you want to go to the "next level," then you should join SAG. From my experience, it's not as steep a climb to join SAG due to the regulations and the amount of work that is available. It's easier to get SAG hours and it's easier to buy into it. Equity can be a bit more challenging to step into because that work isn't nearly as prevalent as film work, for obvious reasons. Just know once you join a union such as Equity, you are in competition with everyone else in the union, as well.

So soprano's, if you're game to go to the same auditions as Tony© Award winners, go for it. If you're not at that level yet, don't curb your chances of being employed because joining Equity will require you to only take Equity contracts. That means all the non-equity opportunities are practically closed to you (with the few exceptions of an Equity Guest Artist Contract or an Equity Waiver). The key is to know when it's the right time for you to jump in. If you're settled in New York and want to make your living there, it's probably a good idea to be union, because all the paying jobs (at least decent ones with a livable salary) will be union. However, just because you are union does not guarantee you'll be able to stay in New York. There are some great union regional theatres that employee solely union actors. However, the competition is just as stiff, because they are hiring from the same pool as any show in New York. If you want to travel around and maybe do a cruise-ship gig or any other venture, it might not be the best time to join.

As for the nature of unions, know exactly what you are signing up for. Yes, they help their constituents make a better way of working and living, but make no mistake, they are also a business and they run as such. This applies to every union.

Once again, I'm using Equity as an example because that's the one I have the most knowledge of. I'll give you 3 examples of what I'm talking about.

First, in 2014 the Equity-League Health Trust Fund, which is the insurance promoted by Actors Equity, made drastic cuts to health benefits for those that didn't meet strict requirements. According to the New York Times in an article published on November 9, 2014[17], the fund provides coverage to about 6,000 Actors' Equity members. Members can qualify for 6 months of coverage if they work a union contract for 12 weeks out of the year, or 12 months of coverage for those that work 20 weeks. Those that didn't meet that requirement were provided with insurance once they exhausted the benefits of a federal insurance law known as Cobra.

If the federal program goes under, the health fund will have to pick up the rest of the insurance. Due to the fact of rising health costs, they modified their system, leaving those that don't meet the requirements (such as older actors and those with long-time illnesses) without insurance. So imagine paying union dues your whole life and putting money in the health fund, only to be cut from the program when you need it. Unfortunately, that's the way of business.

The second example is a recent embattlement with LA based theatres operating under the Equity 99-seat plan. In short, many small theatres in LA were doing new and experimental work, in which many of the theatres were owned by members of the union, and were using mostly volunteer-based union actors. The union decided that everyone working in these theatres should be paid at least $9/hour and put it up for a vote within the union. Many members said that financial strain would be too much on these small theatres and that their main goal was not to make money, but to have a place to do new works. Due to the financial strain of owning and renting property in LA, as well as, production costs, the theatres and their actors were working on a largely volunteer basis in order to produce new art.[18]

The local actors voted against the new rule by a 2-1 margin, however, Actor's Equity decided to go ahead and make the increase mandatory anyway. Considering the fact that union put the new rule up to a vote and the vote was strongly against it, it shows the union can be more concerned with its own business than the members it represents. I'm not saying the union doesn't care about its members, but what I am saying is that it also has its own business affairs it must work around. This isn't just unique to Actor's Equity, you can find examples of this in every union you come across.

The last example I have is that of a double-standard. When you join Equity, you are told that you may not take any non-union jobs, in no uncertain language. According to Equity's website, "working without a contract seriously diminishes Equity's ability to stimulate professional work opportunities, undercuts all other agreements, creates unfair competition, and it's ultimately detrimental to the welfare of all the members."[19] If you join a union, it would make sense that you wouldn't be allowed to take non-union jobs. Otherwise, what's the point of joining? However, you would not expect an elected official of the union to be involved with a non-union production, would you? Of course not.

I was music directing for a major cruise line (a non-union entity) and one of the director/choreographers was one of Actors Equity's elected officials. Out of respect, I will withhold the name. Yes, directors and choreographers are not covered under Equity. However, it always seemed like a double standard to me that an elected official of Equity was directing a non-union show. How is it that the same person that represents the union that demands its members not to work outside the union can support and direct a non-union production? It just goes to show that everyone will bend the rules, either legal or moral, to make money in this business.

So, what's the moral of all of this? Know when joining a union is right for you. Even though unions are there to protect you, make sure you also protect yourself, because I promise you, the union will always protect itself.

NEGOTIATING AND CONTRACTS

The definition of a contract is an agreement on paper for the amount of work verses compensation and under what terms that is achieved. Contracts don't have a lot of leeway, so you had better make sure you know what you are singing before you put your name on it. And remember, contracts are only as good as the people who make them.

Two of the biggest problems most people have when negotiating contracts are 1) they are afraid to ask for what they want and 2) they have a difficult time talking about money. These are two fears you have to get over and with the advice in this section, I'll give you some actionable steps you can take to curb this fear and achieve what you want.

So before you negotiate anything you need to ask yourself 3 questions:

- What do you want?

- Why do you want it?

- How much do you want it for?

These questions seem pretty simple, but you must answer them thoroughly. They are the foundation of negotiating and without full and annotated answers to each, you will not have the foundation (leverage) to negotiate.

So the first question, "What do you want?", is the overall "perfect outcome" of what you want out of a contract. Write down how much money you want, if you want a travel stipend, a living per diem, or housing. I personally do not take a contract unless they pay for my housing and travel, as these are hands down the largest expenses you will have, and it will eat into your salary very quickly.

You must then know why you want it, or better yet, why you

deserve that. For example, if you live in North Carolina and you find a gig in Florida for a couple of weeks, it's not out of the realm of reason to ask for travel and housing. A good rule of thumb is if the gig is more than two hours from your home, ask for travel reimbursement. Since you'll be in Florida for only a couple of weeks, finding a short-term lease or a longer hotel stay can be very expensive, so make sure the people hiring you pay for your housing, as well. Even if they pay you $1,500 a week, and you have to provide your own travel and housing, that's close to 75% of your salary. That's not including taxes and living expenses. It's just not a viable option. Because of these factors, you have leverage to ask for these.

And third, you have to know how much you want it for. So how do you establish what to ask for? Do some research to find the best asking price. How much is the price of living where you're going? It's going to be cheaper living in rural Georgia than it will be in Miami. How much experience do you have? If you've built up your résumé, your salary should reflect that. How much are you going to be working? Is the amount they are paying you comparable to the amount of hours you will be working? Also, ask around for people that have worked at that venue before or if anyone knows anything about it. You can pick up very valuable information from your colleagues.

With all this gathered information, give yourself a budget of what your daily and monthly expenses are and adjust that number with the information you've gathered. A clearer picture of what you will need to ask for will form.

One simple thing people tend to forget about, in business and in life, is that you need to establish your self-worth. This is the driving force behind every decision you make. If you do not tell people how much you are worth, you allow someone else to establish it for you and you will be valued way less than you truly are.

Many performers and technicians, from amateurs to seasoned professionals, will take low paying contracts that require them to work six days a week, 8-10 hour days. After they do the math on how much they are paid verses the time worked, they realize they weren't even paid minimum wage. Unfortunately, there are several theatres and different venues that do not offer livable wages. You can't even compare them to working as a burger flipper because they actually make more.

So by this logic, you have to know how much you need to live and what you need to be paid per day to make that work. Be sure not to short change yourself because you're afraid of losing a job. I've never heard of a company withdrawing an offer because someone asked for more money. And if they do, you probably don't want to work for them in the first place. Oftentimes companies will respect you more because they know you hold yourself to a higher value (which goes back to question 2). People will only value you as much as you value yourself.

Think about that principle from a different perspective. If you go to buy a car and one car is $500 and the other is $25,000, which one are you going to say is the better car? The $25,000 one, of course. Why? Because it may be newer, or have better parts, and the price reflects its value. So why would you sell a car that's worth $25,000 for any less? You wouldn't do it because it doesn't make any sense. So why should we be judged any differently? You are selling a product and you don't want to devalue it (i.e. yourself).

Now that we've covered the foundation of negotiation, let's look at more of the "how to" part of it.

I think one of the best models of selling and negotiating is by Jordan Belfort, aka, "The Wolf of Wall Street." He founded and ran one of the most successful investment firms in the country during the 1980's. He was a master in sells and in negotiating multi-million dollar deals. In his primetime, he was making up to one million dollars a week using these four simple adjectives: sharp, enthusiastic, authoritative, and positive.[20] Now let's break each one of these down and see how they apply to you.

First, you must walk into the room sharp as a tack. Before you even start any discussions on a potential contract you must gather intelligence. You need to find out about that theatres/ company's history. You should find out about everyone that is in an administrative role there and their history and how they came into that position. You need to find out as much information as you can, so that before you walk into the room you have a nearly complete picture of the show/product, as well as, company that is looking to hire you. This way, you can find common connections between you and the theatre, and have talking points to help build rapport with the people signing your contract. Remember, people love working with friends. A good rule of thumb is, if you don't know who the sucker in the room is, it's you. Don't be the sucker. Be prepared with so much knowledge they can't help but take notice of you.

Second, you must be enthusiastic. Enthusiasm is contagious and will help with the negotiating process. Essentially what you are doing when you approach something with enthusiasm is to manipulate the other person with your energy. Emotional thoughts are much stronger than rational thoughts, so when you get someone involved with your enthusiasm, you are engaging them emotionally and that will make them much more receptive to give you what you want. When you're demonstrating that you're passionate about what you do and what you're really good at, you're making them buy into your value that will, in turn, increase the value of the company and the project they're working on.

The third thing you need to embrace is your ability to be authoritative. This is where most people go awry. Ironically, most artists I've met over the years have great confidence in themselves and in their abilities, but that confidence goes out the window when it comes to business and asking for what they really want. This goes back to knowing your self-worth. In order to get what you want out of your career, business, and in life you must hold your own presence, listen fiercely, and talk only when needed. So when you ask for something, don't apologize for it and make sure you can back it up. Stand by your requests and let them come up to you and match your level. That's what holding your ground is and it produces results.

And finally, be positive. Go in with a good attitude and make them want to like you. After all, like I've said many times before, everyone loves working with their friends. You might as well make some new ones along the way. Who is to say business just has to be about business?

Now, with these four things in mind, your first goal is to put your research to work. This is why being sharp is important and doing your research beforehand gives you the upper hand. You need to be the one in charge of the conversation, and the one in charge of the conversation is the one asking the questions. Ask them about the company and how they operate and some of the history behind it. Because of the research you've done beforehand, you can ask intelligent insightful questions most people could not. This automatically makes you stand out, and it helps you fill in the gaps of your research so that you can now have a complete picture of the company and your job.

They will often give you a run down of the history of the company, what type of people they are looking for, and they will go into the specifics of what they will offer you; such as, housing, pay, and travel. Make sure you listen intently and remember what they are saying. Try not to talk too much during this, just be a sponge. Even if what they are saying doesn't quite match up with what you want, just continue to listen. The part where you ask for "what you want" comes later.

A good thing to remember during this part of the conversation is that when they are talking about the company and its members/employees to you, they are selling that company to you. This puts you in the power position, which is good because you want to be authoritative. You want to hold onto the power position as long as possible by letting them sell the company to you and then steering them to where you want to go.

At this point, after they have finished talking about the company and the specifics of the job, in your mind you should be thinking about how their offer compares to what you want. Some points will line up, while others won't.

After they have finished talking, they will ask you what your thoughts are. You must remember to be authoritative and positive. In a question format, ask them if they can match what you want. For example, if they offer you housing but with a shared room and bathroom, your response could sound like this, " I'm definitely interested in the job, however, is there any way you can provide a private room with a bath?" Many times, they will try to accommodate your request or meet you halfway. They might say they can give you a private room but not a private bath. That's doable because the most important aspect of a private bedroom is covered, and you can compromise on the bathroom.

Once you establish housing, travel, meal per diems, and any other things necessary for living, it's time to move on to money. Always save money for last. There are two reasons. The first being, if you can get them to say "yes" to the easy stuff, such as travel, it's easier to get a "yes" on the amount of money you ask for. This is the same principle of controlling other people's reactions by controlling your actions. If someone says "no" right out of the gate, it's hard to get a yes later on. However, people are wired to be more agreeable if you start off positive, such as, getting them to say "yes" to something easy like a travel stipend. It's the snowball effect, one "yes" begets more "yeses."

The second reason to leave money for last is that if you compromised earlier, as in the private bedroom example, they will believe you will work with them to find common ground. However, the trick here is to lead them to where you want to go, so you aren't really compromising at all. Here's an example to show you how to do just that:

The trick in money negotiating is to ask for 10-15% *more* than what you *actually* want. The reason I say 10-15% is because if you want $1,200/week, then asking for $1,320 doesn't seem that outrageous. If you negotiate with this principle, you will have one of three outcomes:

The first, and the best, is that they give you $1,320 a week.

Congratulations, you got a raise. The second outcome is that they will negotiate it down 10-15% to $1,200 a week, which is exactly what you wanted in the first place. And the third outcome, they will say "no" to both and go back to their original offer. At this point, you make a judgment call whether or not you want to take the job. But never forget your self-worth. Don't sell yourself short.

One of my favorite quotes about this very situation is from Warren Buffett, one of the wealthiest people in the world. He was speaking to Jimmy Buffett, who had asked him about a deal that was proposed with a major entertainment company. The company was asking a lot from Jimmy Buffett, but it also would have made him a decent amount of money. He wasn't sure if he should take the deal or not. Warren Buffett then said to him, "Whether you make or don't make this deal, is it going to affect your life? And if not, then do what you want to do and be prepared for them to say no."[21]

Essentially what he is saying is this, don't be afraid to ask for what you want but have a backup if they say no. However, don't sell yourself short by getting into something that will not make you happy and fulfilled. Once again, it's knowing your self-worth and sticking to it.

A great example of this happened to a colleague of mine a few years back. He too is a music director and was looking to pick up more contracts. He had one recurring contract that he had been on for over five years, but they were asking him to do more shows without a pay raise. While in renegotiating the recurring contract, he began to look for another opportunity in case his recurring one didn't come through. He wanted to make sure he had a backup plan, as well as, leverage.

He found another venue looking for a music director, as well as, an artistic director. After talking with the executives there, he realized that both of those positions weren't very defined and neither had a large workload. He then began to negotiate with the new venue about combining both of those jobs and combining the salary and letting him take over. He originally only wanted to find a backup plan in case his recurring contract didn't want to renegotiate his terms. But now he could use the new offer as leverage because of the job and price increase.

At the end, his recurring contract did decide to renegotiate (because they realized they would loose him if they didn't), but the job he created for himself at the new venue ended up offering him more money and benefits. After he established himself at the new venue, he negotiated to take a month and half off to do his recurring contract. He only accomplished this because of the leverage he created for himself. So in the end, if he only got one contract, he would still be covered. However, both venues recognized his worth, and he now works for both of them at a premium of what his salary originally was.

He used the tools I described above, and with the proper leverage, he got exactly what he wanted. You have the same ability to do it yourself. You just have to trust yourself that you can and that you are worth it. Establish your self-worth and everyone else will follow suit.

FINANCIAL PLANNING

Okay, before you close the book thinking that I'm going to be getting into hard-core economics, I'm going to assure you it's going to be okay and I'm not going to be talking about 401(k)'s and IRA's and everything else in-between. However, I will give you some easy, quick tips that are both actionable and measureable that will help you maintain longevity in this business.

Financial planning is hands down the best way to find success in this business. Having the proper financial planning can mean the difference between an extraordinarily talented person dropping out because they couldn't make ends meet, and someone with decent talent making it all the way to the top. The difference is the second person had the financial means to stick it out to the very end; which brings me to the first and most important insight about money.

Wealth is measured in time, not in the amount of money. This may seem a little abstract to some, but I will try to break it down so that you get the idea behind it. Think about it this way: If a woman is worth $15 million dollars and spends $1 million a day, she is a very poor woman because she will be broke in two weeks. But if the same woman worth $15 million dollars spends $200 a week, she can live off that money for 1,422 years. She, therefore, is an extremely wealthy woman. It is the control that she has over her money that makes her wealthy.

Here's a more practical example of how wealth is measured in time. Think about cars, trains, and planes. Imagine you're going on a trip from Raleigh, North Carolina to New York City. If you take a car, which is the cheapest way, it takes you about nine hours and a couple of tanks of gas. If you take a train, it's a little more expense but you get there in about seven hours. If you take a plane, which is the most expensive, you can be there in an hour and a half. What you are doing is literally buying time. The same rule applies to your finances. The more money you save and spend with restraint, the more time you have.

You have to be in complete control of your money, otherwise, it will get totally out of hand. Money can be a highly emotional subject for many people, but if you can learn to take the emotion out of it and think with more rationality, your finances will greatly improve.

So your first goal is to get out of debt. This includes consumer debt (such as, your credit cards) and student loan debt. The best method to do this is using the snowballing technique. Essentially what this does is help you build up your monthly payments by paying off the smaller debts and using the money left after paying them off to attack the larger debts. Here is an example of this method in action:

Say you have three major debts to pay off: a $3,000 credit card bill (with a $65 minimum payment), a $600 medical bill ($55 minimum), and your $10,000 worth of student loans (which is a $100 minimum). What you do is line these up from smallest to largest. So you'll pay off the medical bill first, then the credit card bill, then your student loans. Don't worry about interest rates, they will mean nothing to you when you get rolling.

So, you start by paying the minimum on all your debts except your medical bill. You go after that one with a vengeance. In order to do this, you need to cut your expenses and try to bring in more money. So, for the time being, don't go to Starbucks every morning and get a coffee. Don't go out to eat every night. Then try to bring in more money, maybe by picking up a small part-time job or using online marketing to bring in a few extra dollars. Remember, as I mentioned earlier in the book, you must be stoic. You give up some pleasures in the beginning in order to have significant gains later on.

Let's say after all of this, you find an extra $400 a month. You're now paying $450 (the $400 you've found plus your $50 minimum) towards your $600 medical bill. That debt won't last much longer than a month. Now take that $450 and apply it to your credit card bill. Since you're already paying $65 on your credit card bill, you'll now have $515 to attack it with. You'll have your credit card bill paid off in 5 ½ months. Now roll that $515 into your student loan, which now gives you $615 ($515 plus $100 minimum) to attack it with. In one year and 6 months, you'll have your $10,000 student loan debt paid off and you'll be debt free. So using this system, you could have paid off $13,600 in combined debt in a little over a year and a half. It just takes discipline and the drive to do it.

Make no mistake about this, money (the amount we have or don't have) is directly related to our behavior. The more disciplined you are, the more money you will have. And the more money you have, the happier you will be because it gives you freedom. It's freedom from debt and the freedom to make choices based on what you want to do and not if you can pay the bills or not. That's not a bad pay off for a little over a year and half of work.

So what do you do now that you're out of debt? You still have to be disciplined, but it becomes exponentially easier. The first thing I would say is to build yourself an emergency fund of about $5,000. Using the money left over after paying your debts, you should be able to build this up rather quickly. This money should be used for a cushion and nothing more. You don't spend this money unless an emergency happens, like you can't pay rent or your car broke down. This money is there to give you peace of mind in case something bad happens.

Once you have established an emergency fund, start by taking your money and splitting it 50/50 into checking and savings. You want to give yourself a cap on how much you keep in checking, so let's say it's $4,000. This way you have a mental and literal cap on what you can spend. If you use it all, that's it. You don't get to dip into your savings.

So let's say you make $1,000 a week. Take $500 and put it in checking and $500 and put it in savings. Do this until you reach your $4,000 cap in your checking account. Once it's reached, you put the remainder in savings or invest it. Here's an example of this: You make $1,000 a week and split it 50/50. That's $500 in each account. Let's assume your living expenses are $200 a week. So each week you should be able to save $300 in checking and $500 in savings. In about three and a half weeks, you'll meet your $4,000 checking cap and have around $6,500 in savings (not including your emergency fund). Once you meet your checking's cap, you'll only need $200 a week to replenish it instead of $500, leaving you $800 a week. With the extra $300 you can either put it in savings or invest it.

There are two types of investments you can make, either in yourself or something that pays dividends such as stocks and bonds. Both investments should make you more money because that's essentially what an investment is: spending money on things that make you more money.

I'm not going to go into asset investment in this book. There are plenty of other people smarter and more versed in stocks/bonds/real estate investment than I am. And the good news is that they also have books on it that you can learn from. A great start would be Robert Kiyosaki's *Rich Dad, Poor Dad*. And no, he doesn't pay me to promote his book; I just believe in it that much, because it's so good. He has a very approachable method to investing that makes sense to ordinary people, so you won't feel like you're reading an economic textbook.

I will, however, go into investing in yourself and your business. Warren Buffett once said, "It's good to learn from your mistakes. It's better to learn from other people's mistakes." There is absolutely no need to go into this business without any sort of guidance. There have been enough people to come before you to make every mistake in the book. Luckily many of them have written their mistakes in a book that you can read for yourself. There isn't any reason you shouldn't know how to build your career in entertainment, because there is enough material out there to guide you. So the first thing you should invest in is yourself and learn skills that will help you promote yourself and your career. So with that extra $300, buy books on marketing or how to be a better businessperson or negotiator. These are tricks that will help you get to the level you want. Take classes and buy books on these subjects. You'll be surprised how much you'll learn. You've already bought this book; so it shows you already have the willingness to learn. Use this as the foundation to build upon. This knowledge will make you more money, and the more you learn, the more you will earn. Really maximize your strengths and minimize your weaknesses.

The next trick after learning how to invest in yourself is learning how to budget. The biggest key to staying successful is creating a budget and sticking with it. You should have two budgets: one personal and one professional. This will help you keep track of expenses and what you really need to be spending your money on, as well as, help with taxes when that part of the year rolls around.

For your personal budget, you need to account for everything you spend money on such as rent, utilities, food, clothes, travel, and entertainment. Really dig deep and write everything down and annotate why you need it. If you can't justify a purchase with anything other than "I just really wanted it," then you need to cut that out of your budget and save your money. You'll be surprised how much money you spend on coffee and drinking binges throughout a week.

A good rule of thumb when it comes to deciding if you're ready and have the means to move somewhere is the rent vs. incoming pay balance. If you (after paying all your debts and have an emergency fund) have enough money coming in one week out of the month to easily pay for your rent and utilities, then you can afford to live at that particular place. Too often people move to high expense areas without the proper foundation. They realize after paying their debts and living expenses it takes them almost the entire month to pay the rest of their bills. This means you have to work backbreaking hours just to be able to live. Not to mention, they are living paycheck to paycheck with absolutely no emergency fund.

Instead, why not take a job, such as a cruise ship, that pays very well. It will also take care of your housing, travel, and expenses and pay off all your debts and build a monetary cushion in which to live. Let me tell you, NY and LA aren't going anywhere and there is no harm in taking a couple of years to prepare yourself. It's foolish to move somewhere like that with no monetary plan and just expect to "wing it." You and I both know people like that. They never really accomplish anything and burn out every time. Don't fall into the trap of thinking, "Oh, if I don't start out in NY right after college, it will be too late and I'll never break into this business!" That is a lie. You'll be much more prepared and make greater strides knowing your finances are in order. That way when you get there, all you have to do is worry about the reason you went to begin with: launching your career with 100% focus.

If you take away one thing from this section remember this: just because someone told you that being an artist and moving somewhere is going to be a constant struggle doesn't make it true. That just means they didn't take the time to research and prepare themselves. That's the defeatist-majority mentality this book is teaching you to go against. Don't fall into that trap, instead be the exception and make people wonder how you did it.

With your personal budget, you'll want to keep it as lean as you can. Cook at home more often, go to TJ Maxx to buy clothes and don't buy them as often, find cheaper ways to travel (taking the subway instead of a taxi), and instead of going to see an Imax movie every week, just watch something on Netflix. Once you trim out all the fat, you'll be shocked at how much money you can save. The key is to stay disciplined and stick with the plan. It will pay dividends in the long run.

Remember, it's Stoic verses Epicureanism. Stoic people put off short-term pleasures for long-term gain. Epicureans are materialistic and want everything in the immediate and end up paying the bill the rest of their lives. You want to work like no other today, so you can live like no other tomorrow. Budgeting will help you achieve that goal. So when everyone else is dropping out of the business because they can't pay bills and it's "too hard," you'll be chugging along with no worries because you prepared for the hardships.

The next budget you have is your professional budget. This budget should include everything from marketing materials, your website, headshots, video reels, classes you may take, to tabs you pick up during business dinners. Even budget in things you don't expect; such as, the costs to get a passport or immunizations you may need if you're asked to travel overseas. Budgeting will help you keep your expenses low and see where you should really be spending your money.

When you do the math for the first time and you see you're spending $800 on headshots and only $150 on getting really nice video reels done, maybe you should rethink how you spend your money. As I talked about earlier in the networking section, plan on picking up the tab every now and again and put that into your budget. On the occasion that your website hosting fees go up, make sure you have enough budgeted and saved that you can cover the difference if needed. The little things can add up to big money, so make sure you have control over every dime that is spent. And the good news, especially if you're working as a contractor, is that almost 90% of those things in your professional budget are tax write-offs.

So, the important thing to take away from this section is this: take control of your money, get out of debt, spend wisely, and invest heavily in yourself and into assets that make you more money. Once you grow your money beyond your monthly expenses, you start to gain financial freedom. That freedom is the greatest one of all, because it leaves you with choice; you no longer have to do anything just because you need the money to survive.

Really spend some time improving your financial literacy, and like I said before, let this be the foundation you build upon. Continue reading on the subject and become well versed on how to make more money. It will help you exponentially in the long run, both personally and professionally. Think about it like a tool in your toolbox. The more tools you have, the better the chance you have of achieving your dreams. Just make the commitment to yourself that you will gain control of your finances today so that you can fully realize your dream tomorrow. It's that simple.

THE TAX MAN AND YOU: THE TAX MAN COMETH

Make no mistake, your biggest enemy isn't everyone else competing in this business, it's not your landlord telling you to pay your rent (which after this book, shouldn't be a problem for you), or your boss threatening your job. No, your biggest enemy is the Tax Man. I capitalized Tax Man so that he seems more like a comic book villain, which is exactly how you should see him.

You need an army to fight against this foe. He will take every dime he can and prey on the ignorance of others. If he can find a way to take some of your money, he will.

Most people complain that they need a pay raise in order to make ends meet and this is a logical fallacy. Now this is not me making a political statement, this is me giving you a different perspective in which to view this subject. When you sign a W2 (the tax form the IRS has you sign when you become someone's employee) you are taxed on the money you make and they take it out of every paycheck. Here's the catch, the more money you make; the more money they take out. And unfortunately, most people aren't as disciplined as you are with their finances, so they think they are making more money and end up spending more. In reality, since their taxes increase with the amount of money they make, they essentially make the same. However, with their increased spending, they end up with less money overall.

Think about this. Have you ever seen those people on TV that win millions in the lottery and after a year they are completely broke? It's because they never learned how to properly contain and spend (invest) money. It has absolutely *nothing* to do with the amount of money they have. Not only that, when they received such a massive sum of money, they were taxed to death on it, sometimes up to 45-50%. That's half of what they made. Then they blew the rest.

So after you have completely removed emotion from your thoughts about money and have gotten a grip on your finances, your real problem is the Tax Man taking away what you've worked hard to earn. So for those people that say, "I need a pay raise to have more money," I say, "No, you need to learn to fight the Tax Man so you can keep the money you have. Then you'll have more money."

So what's step one in fighting the Tax Man? Hire an accountant. And I'm not talking about having your uncle or your cousin do it, and I'm definitely not telling you to let H&R Block do it. I'm telling you to hire a private CPA that owns their own accounting firm. This is for a number of reasons:

First, when you hire a private accountant, they have a special interest in really helping you get the most out of your taxes. The reason they have a special interest is because they own that business. They pay for the building they're in and they want to keep people happy. Unlike H&R Block (and companies that are similar), you're dealing with employees of the company, and if they really help you or not is of no concern to them. They just want to get their paycheck and leave. However, the private CPA wants his clients to always stick around, so they work harder to do your finances correctly and get you as much money back as possible. Yes, they may be a bit more expensive, but I would rather pay a private CPA $400 to do my taxes and have to pay $200 to the IRS than have some regular employee or relative do them for free and have to pay $1,200 to the IRS.

The second reason I vouch for a private CPA is the need to stay on top of constantly changing tax laws. There are tax breaks and certain advantages to different professions. It's imperative to find someone that is familiar with your line of work and the tax laws that apply to you. When you are an artist, there are certain "loopholes" that are available to you and you want someone that can use every trick to your advantage. When you go somewhere like an H&R Block, they hand their employees packets with that years new tax breaks and they treat everyone the same. It's a very "cookie cutter" way of doing taxes, and the absolute best way to waste your money.

Take some time and familiarize yourself with how the tax laws affect you. I'm not talking about learning everything about tax laws, but you can go to the IRS website and look up what tax laws apply to your profession. Just read over it and gather some intelligence for yourself. It gives you more control so you aren't totally handing the reins over to someone else. It's just like buying a car, you don't just take the mechanic's word for it 100%, you do some research so you can ask intelligent questions before buying and see if he's being totally honest or not. Give yourself some protection by researching so you have some working knowledge.

A good trick I've learned to help you keep up with your expenditures is to keep track of your bank statements, instead of your receipts. Using your debit card (*not* your credit card, remember debt's your enemy) to make everyday purchases instead of cash is easier to keep up with if you're disciplined.

So instead of every month sitting at your desk counting receipts, just print off your bank statements. They will have every purchase you made in chronological order, as well as, where and how much you spent. Then highlight and annotate every business expense. I suggest doing this at the end of every month. It's easier to annotate your expenses from two weeks ago, than it is to remember what you spent money on seven months ago.

If you take cash out of the ATM, just have a little piece of paper in your wallet to note what you're using that money for. The more thorough you are with your records, the easier it is to file your taxes later.

Another perk to having your purchases in chronological order on your bank statements is that if you travel away from your taxable home, many purchases become deductibles that normally wouldn't be. For example, if you live in Florida and get a three-month gig in Virginia, there are certain allowances the government lets you deduct daily on food and lodging. This is because if you had to move from your taxable home (the address on your driver's license) to work elsewhere your expenses would greatly increase. So when you see your bank statement, you can highlight from January to March when you were out of state and many of those everyday items become deductibles.

In addition to this, you want to keep your residency in the cheapest state possible. If you're from Florida and you move to NYC, keep your residency in Florida because when it comes to paying taxes, Florida income tax is significantly cheaper than New York state tax. This will save you thousands of dollars.

Now there are two types of forms that will apply to you, the W2 and the W9. The W2 form is your most standard form. Every time you become an employee and are put on payroll, you sign a W2. This takes out federal, state, social security, and Medicare taxes. People that work under W2 are often times taxed the heaviest.

The W9 is the tax form for independent contractors. This means you are paid in a lump sum (or payments over the course of your contract, depending on how it's set up) and you pay taxes on all of it at the end of year. Most people will say they want taxes taken out every paycheck so they don't have to worry about it at the end of the year and this is a critical mistake. Those working under W2 do not have all of the tax benefits of someone working under a W9. So in reality, you can make more money under a W9, write off more business expenses than someone working with a W2, and pay fewer taxes. The key here is to be disciplined to have enough money at the end of the year to pay your taxes. Do you see a pattern between money and discipline? Yes, you may pay $1,200 on taxes at the end of the year under a W9, but if you look at the taxes taken out of your weekly W2, you'll notice you've paid significantly more over the course of a year. You just didn't notice because it's been taken out in smaller chunks. So whenever possible, always work under a W9.

The items you can write off as an artist can vary just like the weather, and I have one rule when it comes to marking deductions to give to your accountant; if you or anyone else has to pay for "it" regardless, don't write it off. This is stuff like buying clothes and getting haircuts. Everyone buys these things regardless if it's for work or not, so it's hard to justify them as a business deduction. However, if you buy more expensive everyday items like a laptop, which you use specifically for work, there can be tax breaks there.

However, there are many things you can write off and justify as business expenses. Here are some examples:

- Mileage (if traveling away from your taxable home)
- Any Travel (plane tickets, train tickets, etc. if business related)
- Food (if traveling away from your taxable home)
- Housing (if you have to pay for housing when away from your taxable home)
- Equipment Purchases (Computers, Pianos, Sound Equipment, etc.)
- Sheet Music
- iTunes Music Purchases (justifiable as research, must be documented)
- Show tickets (justifiable as research, must also be documented)
- Books (justifiable as business research, must be documented)
- Business Dinners (If you paid for a dinner between colleagues and discussed business, must be documented)

The key here is to find things than you can realistically relate to your business and mark them as deductions. Once again, you must document these purchases. So in addition to keeping all your bank statements, also keep a journal of purchases related to your business (sheet music, iTunes, show tickets, etc.) and how much each thing costs and what you used it for. Just in case you are ever asked, you have documentation of why you purchased it and how much you spent on it.

Be smart about your finances and don't try to write-off getting a new puppy as a business expense. That will throw up red flags. The best thing to take away from this section is hire an accountant and help them get the best tax return for you. If you stay on top of your purchases and keep good records of what you spend and why, it will save you lots of time and money at the end of the year.

YOUR DAY JOB

Your day job is a means to an end. That's one of the most important things you can ever remember. *Your day job is a means to an end.* Your day job should be nothing more than a vehicle to take you to where you want to go. Think about it as a temporary lifeboat. You use it to keep you afloat and you want to get off of it as soon as you can. If you stick by the advice in this book and change your thinking so that you can be on top of your financial planning, that dream can come true sooner than you think.

Too often people move to a new place to pursue their dreams and say, "I'm going to get a day job and then work during my time off to accomplish my goals." Then they get stuck in the job, often working 10-12 hour days, just to pay bills. They become completely consumed by trying to survive that they forget the whole reason they moved there in the first place. That's the equivalent of dropping your lifeboat in the middle of a hurricane and "wingin' it."

These same people work everyday and then justify it to themselves that it's okay to become complacent and not make any strides towards their dreams. Your day job should be a vehicle that pushes you to work harder and make strides to your goals. Everyday you should wake up and make a plan on how you're going to be successful enough to leave your day job behind and never look back.

While you're working your day job, you need to set aside time to evaluate your progress on the goals you've set for yourself. Then you need to come up with an action plan on how you plan to achieve those goals and actually follow through with it. I see too many people in the city when I go visit that are completely void of any drive. Not because of the city, but because they've totally lost sight on what they went there to accomplish. I ask them how they are doing and they always reply, "I'm just surviving man..." What?! That's not a way to live! We are not meant to become complacent and just work to survive. That's the opposite of the good life. So use that energy as fuel to make your dreams a reality. Strive to be the person when asked how you are doing that responds, "I'm great and I'm getting it done!"

If you find yourself in a job that barely pays enough to take care of your expenses, a job that requires you to work 10-12 hour days, six days in a row, you need to quit that job immediately and find one that will give you the time to pursue your goals. Don't stop until you do. Remember, use it as fuel to get you farther.

I knew of one girl that wanted to pursue a career in commercial dance. She had it all. She was gorgeous, an amazing dancer, and an even better person. However, she moved to LA and quickly got a day job in a popular clothing store. She worked crazy hours just to get her bills paid. Because she had a great work ethic, they promoted her to manager. This was a relief because that meant a pay raise so she could make ends meet without working so many hours. She became so comfortable and complacent; she stopped working towards her goal. She eventually became very depressed and couldn't get out of her funk. After some time she realized she had backed herself into a corner and that she needed to pursue her career head-on. She made a plan and saved enough money to float her for a little while, and she quit her job and focused on making her dance career happen. Within a couple of months, she filmed several music videos and is now a backup dancer for several upcoming artists. She believed in herself, made a plan, and made it happen.

So what's the moral of this story? Your goals are more important than your day job. This may sound radical to a lot of you. But if you ever want to be happy and be completely fulfilled, you have to trust in yourself and take the leap. Remember, if you're getting a paycheck, you are making someone else's dream a reality. So you might as well take that time to make yours a reality instead.

I'm sure you're wondering why I am telling you this. That I'm probably from a family where I had everything taken care of, so it's easy for me to say. But I'm here to tell you quite the opposite is true. I wouldn't give advice that I don't live myself. I've worked hard for every thing that I have now and was able to do it on my own accord. It is scary to take that jump and just trust that you have the ability to make it happen. But I'm here to tell you that you do. It's all in your mind. You just have to believe it. This same advice has taken me across the world, let me open for major musical acts, music direct for well known performers, become friends with people I thought I would never meet, and write this book to help other people along their way. Don't ever forget your goals, they are what make you, "you." And, when it comes to your day job, I'll give you a piece of advice that my dear friend, Maddie, learned from her father and then gave to me: "You can always get another $20, but you can never get another 20 minutes."

CLOSING

Working Artist, Starving Artist

The New Business of Show Business

THE STEP OUT

"Come to the edge, he said..."

- Christopher Logue

C ontrary to popular belief, there are three sides to every coin: heads, tails, and the edge. Wisdom and knowledge are only found on the edge. In order for you to be successful in any facet of life, you have to be able to see both sides of the coin. Many people get caught in the trap of only seeing one side of a problem; their side. What they fail to realize is that if they put their own agenda aside and saw what the other side needed, their problems wouldn't seem so insurmountable.

What do I mean by that? Too often people shroud their judgment because they see things from the wrong perspective. Think about it this way. If you go to the Empire State Building on a foggy day and look straight up from the sidewalk, you might be able to see about half way up the building until the rest disappears. However, if you go to the top of the Empire State Building during that same foggy morning and look down, you can see all of New York. The lesson here is don't feel discouraged or insignificant to the point you feel helpless. All you need to do is change your perspective.

That's the secret to all of this. You, and you alone, judge how you see the world, and how you view the world directly affects how it treats you. So don't feel like you're some fresh new artist at the bottom of the totem pole. Don't feel like you're a designer that has no credits hoping someone will give you a chance. Instead, give yourself some worth and innovate out of that situation by changing your perspective. I've given you the tools in this book. Use it as a foundation to build upon and continue growing.

Hopefully this book has opened your eyes to the "other side of the table." Once you know your place in the game and know how the system works, you can make it work for you. Don't be the type of person that says, "Oh, I can't do that. There are too many people auditioning," or "I'll never get that position, there are people way more qualified than I am." That's poor thinking. Be the person that instead says, "I may not be there now, but I'm going to figure out how to make it happen, whatever it takes because I know I have the strength and ability to do it."

I'm here to tell you, there is no magic bullet. There is no secret that truly successful people are trying to keep from you. It truly is determination, perspective, and the willingness to say you don't know it all and to think outside the box.

So, after this change of perspective and new information, what is your goal? Remember, it has to be actionable and measurable. Once you establish your goals, take the principles and advice in this book and apply them to every situation you go into, and you will find success in them. That is a promise I make to you and a promise you should make to yourself.

And remember in your pursuit of goals, everything you do is about the people. I cannot emphasize this enough. Anything in life that's worth anything is about people. So make sure, once you do find your level of success, that you pay it forward. Too often people take for granted those that helped them along the way and never pay the favor in return. This business is hard enough as it is; don't make it harder by trying to go at it alone.

Make sure you treat everyone with respect, because how you treat them will directly effect what comes back to you. I've worked with some amazing pianists over the years and make no mistake; they can make or break your audition just by how you treat them.

I've known people to come into an audition and begin to sing in the key of "why bother" and the pianist would change key mid-song to match them, just because they treated them with such respect. I've also known people that were inherently rude to the pianist that began to go flat and he left them high and dry.

You have to be nice to everyone. And I don't mean faking nice. I mean be a genuine person and try to be friends with everyone. People love working with their friends. This will pay dividends in the long run for you both personally and professionally.

Henry Rollins, a well-known musician, author, and radio personality said it best, "Listen to the stage manager and get on stage when they tell you to. No one has time for your rock star bullshit. None of the techs backstage care if you're David Bowie or the milkman. When you act like a jerk, they are completely unimpressed with the infantile display that you might think comes with your dubious status. They were there hours before you building the stage, and they will be there hours after you leave tearing it down. They should get your salary, and you should get theirs."

Always remember to be humble, gracious, and kind. And for God's sake always keep a sense of humor. It will help you get through just about anything.

So take this with you and build upon it. Don't ever feel like you're inadequate or that you're not talented. Those are lies you taught yourself and you can undo them. Don't ever feel overwhelmed or lost; just remember to stick to your goals and work everyday to achieve them. And never feel scared, the antidote to feeling scared is work. Work towards your goals with a laser-like focus. You'll realize with the perspective this book has given you and your innate drive, you'll be head and shoulders above everyone else. And most importantly, never give up. Your dreams are valid and they will come to fruition.

You read this book. That tells me you're already making progress. I'll leave you with one of my favorite quotes of all time from the English poet Christopher Logue, "Come to the edge', he said. 'We are afraid', they said. 'Come to the edge', he said. They came to the edge, he pushed them and they flew."

APPENDICES

Working Artist, Starving Artist

The New Business of Show Business

ACKNOWLEDGEMENTS

Without the help of these amazing people, this book would have never happened. So from the bottom of my heart, thank you. I hope I have done your stories and wisdom justice and that your collective effort will help thousands more that will follow in your footsteps.

Maddie Casto – Thank you for always being a soundboard for my ideas and helping me get my thoughts in order. You really are my personal guru and I love you for it.

Brooke Quintana – To one of the sweetest and most giving people I've ever met. You really bent over backwards to help me out and I will forever be grateful for it. You amaze me at what you've accomplished thus far and I'm excited to see where you go next.

Chris Minor – Your input on this book really helped me clear up all of the "gray areas" I wouldn't see. Your ideas and input are invaluable. You're one of those people I know I can always get the truth from whether it be good, bad, or indifferent. For that, I'm forever grateful and I love you for it.

Amber Sweet – Thank you for your feedback and enthusiasm

with this project. You're such a positive energy and your insight really helped shape this book.

Chuck Davis – To one of the coolest and most badass people I've ever met, thank you. You've been a great friend and confidant to me over the years, and I appreciate it more than you know. Here's to Key West.

Landon Summers – Thank you for always being willing to help me out and just going with my crazy ideas pretty much blindly. And, thank you for always asking me questions to understand the other side of the story. You are the man for it.

Von Lewis – To a truly great entertainer, one of the best I've ever met. Thank you for helping me come up with the idea to write this book in the first place.

Keith Boyd – Thank you for helping me out at the drop of dime and always being there when I need you. Also, thank you for letting me pay you in burgers and beer.

Angelina Doyle, Tim Maddox, and Zach Cummins – Thank you for helping me get my video project together. If it weren't for your contributions, it would have never happened.

Faye Phillips – Thank you for being so patient with me while editing this book. You're a great friend and I appreciate you more than you know.

Jeff and Sherry Griffin – For always being supportive and putting up with your crazy, globe-trotting son. I love you both.

BIBLIOGRAPHY

1. "Jimmy Buffett Uncut." *60 Minutes*. CBS. 19 Feb. 2005. Television.

2. Fierman, Dan. "Bill Murray on Ghostbusters 3, Get Low, Ron Howard, and Kung Fu Hustle." *GQ*. GQ, 18 July 2010. Web. 21 Nov. 2015.

3. *Johnny Carson: King of Late Night*. Dir. Peter Jones and Mark Catalena. Perf. Johnny Carson. PBS, 2012. TV Documentary.

4. Hill, Napoleon. *Think and Grow Rich*. New York, NY: Jeremy P. Tarcher/Penguin, 2008. Print.

5. "Mel Fisher." *Wikipedia*. Wikimedia Foundation, n.d. Web. 21 Nov. 2015

6. Kiyosaki, Robert T., and Sharon L. Lechter. *Rich Dad, Poor Dad: What The Rich Teach Their Kids About Money-- That The Poor and Middle Class Do Not!* New York: Warner Business, 2000. Print.

7. Lopez, Tai. "Why I Read a Book a Day (and Why You Should Too): The Law of 33% | Tai Lopez |

TEDxUBIWiltz." *YouTube*. Tedx Talks, 15 Jan. 2015. Web. 21 Nov. 2015.

8. Lee, Bruce. "Facebook Page - Bruce Lee." *Bruce Lee*. Facebook, n.d. Web. 21 Nov. 2015.

9. Piper, Watty, and Loren Long. *The Little Engine That Could*. New York: Philomel, 2005. Print.

10. Strouse, Charles, Martin Charnin, and Thomas Meehan. *Annie - The Musical*. 1977. Theatre.

11. "Money 101: Q&A with Warren Buffett." Interview by Aaron Task. *Yahoo! Finance*. Yahoo!, 8 Apr. 2013. Web. <http://finance.yahoo.com/news/money-101--q-a-with-warren-buffett-140409456.html>.

12. Drucker, Peter F. *Managing Oneself*. Boston, MA: Harvard Business, 2008. Print.

13. Johnson, Sam, and Chris Marcil. "The Limo." *How I Met Your Mother*. Dir. Pamela Fryman. CBS. 19 Dec. 2005. Television.

14. Schwartz, Stephen. *Defying Gravity*. Wicked: The Musical. Decca Broadway, 2003. MP3.

15. Carnegie, Dale. *How To Win Friends and Influence People*. New York: Simon and Schuster, 1981. Print.

16. "Actors' Equity Association Benefits." *Actorsequity.org | Actors' Equity Association Benefits*. Actors Equity, n.d. Web. 21 Nov. 2015.

17. Swarns, Rachel L. "A Veteran Actor's Backstage Fight for Affordable Health Care." *New York Times* 9 Nov. 2014, N.Y. ed., Region sec.: n. pag. *Nytimes.com*. 9 Nov. 2014. Web.

18. Ng, David. "Actors in Los Angeles File Lawsuit against Actors' Equity over Wage Hike." *LA Times* 19 Oct. 2015, Arts and Culture sec.: n. pag. *Latimes.com*. 19 Oct. 2015. Web.

19. "Actors' Equity Membership Responsibilities." *Actorsequity.org | Actors' Equity Association Membership*. Actors Equity, n.d. Web. 21 Nov. 2015.

20. Belfort, Jordan, and Abhinav Gulyani. "Jordan Belfort - Straight Line Persuasion System." *Jordan Belfort - Straight Line Persuasion System*. N.p., n.d. Web.

21. Wolfe, Alexandra. "The Last Word: Jimmy Buffett." *Mens Journal* Aug. 2001: n. pag. *Www.mensjournal. com*. Aug. 2001. Web.

22. "Michael Jordan." *Wikipedia*. Wikimedia Foundation, n.d. Web. 15 Dec. 2015.

23. "Facebook." *Wikipedia*. Wikimedia Foundation, n.d. Web. 15 Dec. 2015.

24. "Touring 102 - Let's Take A Look At The Business Model Of Touring | Actors' Equity Association." *Touring 102 - Let's Take A Look At The Business Model Of Touring | Actors' Equity Association*. Actors Equity, n.d. Web. 15 Dec. 2015.

25. "Production Rulebook (League)." Agreements. Actors Equity, 26 Sept. 2011. Web. <https://www.actorsequity. org/docs/rulebooks/Production_Rulebook_ League_11-15.pdf>.

Define Your Success....
Join The Starving Artist Global Community©!

STARVING ARTIST

C O M P A N Y

www.starvingartistcompany.com

Start to define your success with one simple step. Join the Starving Artist Community© at **www.starvingartistcompany.com**! Connect, collaborate, and learn with like-minded artists who are dedicated to advancing their art — just like you!

When you join the Starving Artist Community you'll enjoy:

- *"The Workshop"* — The best online educational tool to help you learn business skills necessary to dominate the show business industry

- *"The Inner Circle"* — Exclusive access to discount premier resources to help take you to the next level of your career

- Live web chats with Tyler and other industry-leading professionals

- Learning first-hand about new releases from the Starving Artist Company©

The Starving Artist Company is dedicated to communicating with you through social media. Make sure to follow our inspiration threads on Instagram©, Twitter©, and Facebook© and enjoy defining your success with the Starving Artist Global Community!

Visit starvingartistcompany.com today and join the Starving Artist Community©!

www.ingramcontent.com/pod-product-compliance
Lightning Source LLC
Chambersburg PA
CBHW051841090426
42736CB00011B/1906